Chaplains In Conflict
The Role of Army Chaplains since 1914

Chaplains In Conflict
The Role of Army Chaplains since 1914

by

Stephen H. Louden
Principal Roman Catholic Chaplain of The British Army

AVON BOOKS
1 Dovedale Studios
465 Battersea Park Road
London SW11 4LR

Chaplains In Conflict was originally an MTh Dissertation, University of Oxford.

The publishers wish to thank the Trustees of the Imperial War Museum for granting their kind permission to reproduce photographic material. All reasonable efforts have been made to trace the provenance of photographs reproduced in this book not contained in the Imperial War Museum archive. Any necessary acknowledgements will be made in future reprints of *Chaplains in Conflict*.

Printed and bound in the U.K.

Avon Books

London
First Published 1996
© Stephen H. Louden 1996
ISBN   1 86033 840 2

To Mary R

Acknowledgements

My special thanks to Veronica Rossi
for her help with the manuscript,
to my fellow Army Chaplains
for their years of friendship and support,
and to the Reverend Michael Elliott
for his encouragement at Westminster College, Oxford.

CONTENTS

Chapter 4
Between The Wars And World War II

Chapter 5
Vietnam And Gulf Chaplains Questionnaire

Chapter 6
Contemporary Army Chaplaincy

Photographs and illustrations
appearing between pages 68 and 69.

Chaplains at the Front:
Rev. E. L. Watson, Senior Baptist Chaplain
Rev. J. M. Simms DD KHC, Presbyterian Principal Chaplain
Bishop Taylor Smith, Chaplain-General
Rev. O. S. Watkins, Senior Wesleyan Chaplain
Rev. E. G. F. Macpherson, Senior Church of England Chaplain

Woodbine Willie (Rev. Geoffrey Studdert Kennedy MC)

Bishop Llewellyn H. Gwynne

Rev. Theodore Bayley Hardy

Rev. Owen Spencer Watkins

Bishop Taylor Smith

Burial in the trenches

Chateau Wood, Flanders, in 1917

A service aboard a troopship

Rev. Arthur Male

Rev. E. J. Kennedy

Sunday Evening Service by A. Michael;
The Bishop of London at the Front

Field Ambulance at Dranoutre

The Last Absolution of the Munsters at Rue du Bois, 1915, by Fortunino Matania

Frederick Llewellyn Hughes: Referent Power

The Venerable Archdeacon W. F. Johnston

Rev. James Harkness

Rev. Dr. Victor Dobbin

The Right Reverend Monsignor Stephen H. Louden
BA DipTh MTh VG

Stephen H. Louden was born at Southport in 1941 and educated at Upholland College before being ordained priest in the diocese of Liverpool. In recent years he attended Westminster College, Oxford, gaining an MTh. He has been Principal Roman Catholic Chaplain and Vicar General of the British Army since 1993. He received his TA commission into the Royal Army Chaplains' Department in 1973 and was subsequently commissioned into the Regular Army in 1978. He has served in Germany, Northern Ireland, Cyprus, Berlin and Hong Kong and was Catholic Chaplain at the Royal Military Academy Sandhurst from 1984-86. He is now based at the Ministry of Defence (Chaplains) at Upavon. He was made a Prelate of Honour in 1993 on his appointment as Principal Roman Catholic Army Chaplain.

INTRODUCTION

This study explores, with particular emphasis on wartime role, how some British army chaplains have perceived their role as ministers of religion within a unique environment. The initial project was to have been a comparison between wartime ministry of US army chaplains in the Vietnam conflict from 1962 to 1974, using the study by Ackerman 1989, and the ministry of the British army chaplains in the Gulf War in 1991. However, the nature and brevity of the war in the Gulf would have invalidated any attempt at a direct role comparison, but rather than jettison the work of three months, which had involved reproducing, sending and analysing by hand a questionnaire sent to the chaplains who had served in the Gulf War identical to the one sent to the chaplains on the US study, a brief comparative analysis has been made between the two surveys in chapter 5.

As relatively little is known by the general public about army chaplaincy the study begins with an overview of the historical link between church and army, leading to the emergence of the Royal Army Chaplains' Department. Its leadership structure is observed with special emphasis on the role of the Chaplain General and the denominational mix within the Department.

The status and role of chaplains is seen both from the viewpoint of the army itself as well as that of the Chaplains' Department. Chaplains are commissioned officers and closely identify with that group both by inclination and status. Rank is seen as one source of role tension. Other anomalies resulting from simultaneous membership of two disparate organizations are reviewed.

Factors determining the role of chaplains in both World Wars are next considered. Emphasis is given to the role in World War I of the Reverend Studdert Kennedy, (Woodbine Willie), who in unashamedly advocating the prevailing patriotic cause hoped by association to further the church's interests. World War I chaplains are shown to have conformed more to the role expected of them by the Army than to have defined a precise role for themselves. In World War II the Reverend Freddy Hughes, subsequently Chaplain

i

General, is revealed from his writing and speeches to have closely identified the aims of the British Army with those of God Himself. The link is made between the attitudes of World War I and World War II chaplains which resulted in varying responses to situations and organizational pressure which led to dysfunctional ministry. The effort made by the Chaplains' Department to retain compulsory church attendance exemplified organizational dysfunction in the use of a military model for church-going, which was in reality a voluntary associational activity.

If the mission of the church as a whole is to communicate the message of Christ to those who are not well acquainted with it, the role of the British army chaplain has been to represent that message in a military context. There is evidence that chaplains rather than attempting to present war as a consequence of human sin and aberration could as a consequence of psychological and social pressures present it as a manifestation of the divine will. The British army chaplains in the Gulf appear on the whole to have attempted to confine their ministry to their core role of ministry of word and sacrament, but many of those institutional pressures well documented in previous longer wars were still operational, threatening to divert chaplains from their ecclesiastical role into serving specifically military aims.

An investigation into those determinants which shaped and continue to shape the role of army chaplains is then pursued in some detail. The activity of chaplains has been very varied both as a consequence of the imprecision of what constitutes their role and the psychological, sociological and organizational pressures put upon them in their attempt to fulfill it within a close, powerful organization. The demands of the army organization, while it does not necessarily subvert the chaplain's religious role, contributes to the alteration of his perception of his role in its own image and likeness. Ideologies are seen to work not in front of our faces, but from behind our backs.

Chapter 1

Role Determinants
of British Army Chaplaincy

The chaplain is a character of no small importance in a
regiment though many gentlemen of the Army think
otherwise. Yet if you are not more successful in the cure
of the soul than the surgeon is in that of the body, I must
confess your 6s 8d a day would be a judicious saving.
You have such hardened sinners to deal with that your
office is a rather ungracious one; but though the officers
and soldiers are in general irreclaimable, the women of
the regiment may perhaps be worked on with better
effect.

(Advice to the Officers and Soldiers of the British Army.
1782 F. Grose)

Sociological studies have shown the overall resemblance of
mainstream churches to other major institutions in society, in that the
interactions within them share basic organizational similarities. The
Royal Army Chaplains' Department though claiming a divine
mission, in the person of its individual chaplains, will be shown at
the micro level to have engaged in many of those activities which
strengthened their standing, authority or power. This opening
chapter is an attempt to analyse some of the components which
shaped the behaviour of individuals within an institution, functioning
within a particular social milieu and in the context of the British
Army at war and peace. Analysis will be grounded at the micro level
where key concepts are seen at work.

Power and Authority

According to a formal theory of authority, the authority which army
chaplains possess has a dual basis, stemming firstly from the Church

from which they were drawn and secondly from the army itself into which they were incorporated as officers and clergymen. This dual authority contained and contains some potential for conflict which will be addressed later. Within the army the chaplain uses the limited authority he is given to shape and control his own environment in the way in which he sees best. One of the reasons why the concentration must be upon the individual chaplain's behaviour at the micro level as opposed to the macro level of the role of the Chaplaincy Department as a whole, can be illustrated most vividly by asking the question whether, for example, an Irish Presbyterian army chaplain would see his own ministry as furthering the aims, objectives and purpose of the Roman Catholic Church or a Roman Catholic Chaplain see his ministry as supporting Irish Presbyterianism, since they both belong to the Army Chaplains' Department. The answer would have to be that it was unlikely in 1992 and as will be shown *a fortiori* in 1914. In other words the individual role of a particular chaplain, except in the most general terms 'to make and sustain Christians', does differ to a degree which will be extensively illustrated. Though, in the popular mind, all chaplains might have been perceived to be doing the same thing within 'The Grand Brotherhood of Chaplains', to use a phrase coined by the Reverend L Hughes, Montgomery's senior chaplain who subsequently became Chaplain General, analysis of favoured activities will demonstrate that the chaplaincy role both from the perspective of chaplains themselves as well as that of Army personnel was very widely interpreted.

One is forced to be aware of a truth clearly stated - that in a large organization top executives may see the organization seeking one kind of state while those in the middle or lower echelons may have dramatically different roles for the organization and for themselves personally.

It is known that informal relationships in an organization can lead to heightened prestige, if not power. Time and again chaplains raised their standing within the army organization by means of informal relationships with Commanding Officers by undertaking the more humdrum duties that would have fallen upon officers of the line, thereby ingratiating themselves with their superiors and fellow officers by being seen to do what was 'useful and practical'. The informal relationship between the Reverend Hughes and Montgomery gave that chaplain enormous prestige which ultimately obtained for him the office of Chaplain General. At every opportunity Hughes included in what he wrote a reference to his own relationship with the Commander by referring to himself as 'General Montgomery's Chief Padre' or by claiming his support. What is significant is that Hughes did this in a way that no other senior officer either needed or chose to do. They enjoyed an organizational authority given them by their rank and appointment. The prestige and power Hughes gained was greatly enhanced by the reiteration of his association with Monty and is an excellent example of a form of Referent Power, which can be defined as the influence B has over C because of B's identification with the very powerful A.

Though the Reverend Hughes is the paradigm of the value of informal relationships in an organization, there can be no doubt that army chaplains were the objects of decreasing prestige throughout the period under review. Not only did the chaplain have no executive authority and whatever power he possessed was based on what some would consider to be superstition or the talismanic element of his role, but he was also in the process of losing the prestige connected with his possession of a specialist role - expert power. Secular deference to their office could still be confused with the belief that they exercised decisive influence. Though the army depended on the spiritual ministrations of the chaplains to the extent that, in their absence, these would scarcely have been provided, the influence which accrued to the possession of what had formerly been seen as a necessary and 'expert' power was continually diminishing. The less importance a soldier gave to religion the less influential was the role of the chaplain over him. There were two counterbalances in favour of the chaplain, viz. the status given him as officer-chaplain and the ability of the church to claim to provide answers in a climate of great confusion.

> To the extent that an environmental pressure is felt by the entire organization and to the extent that one department can deal with that uncertainty, that organizational unit has power. (Hodge & Anthony 1988:385)

Power can be seen then both as an individual as well as a departmental concept. The power of individual chaplains as well as the Church at large can appear to provide stability in contrast with the uncertainty engendered by war as it affected the army.

Conflicts and Tensions

A source of conflict could arise when the interests of the Chaplains' Department in the person of the individual chaplain were challenged by the interests of the Army as an organization. It is the resolution of this conflict by adjusting his behaviour better to suit the demands of his military social milieu that the evidence of this study will appear to support.

During any war the most alluring word is peace and the word peace has often been a stock in trade of the Christian minister. Augustine himself said that the ultimate object of war was peace. One tragedy of the First World War was that the prevailing ecclesiastical view in England embodied the theological aberration transforming the unjust aggressor of Belgium into the embodiment of the spirit of Satan. The Allies were represented as engaging in a war against the Antichrist and as Marrin (1974:219) vividly declared, 'Quite early in the struggle Allied war aims took on apocalyptic overtones' and, because the reality bore no relationship to the grotesque misrepresentation, frustration was an inevitable outcome.

The core conflict for chaplains ranged around the nature of the war itself. Compromise was ruled out by those who described the war in apocalyptic terms. Not that each individual chaplain systematically proceeded towards the same conclusion, but as in every age there were few chaplains who were of sufficiently independent mind to oppose the accepted wisdom that a negotiated peace would be to commit treason against God, sin by bargaining

4

with the Devil, and, most powerfully of all, betray the sacrifice of those who had already fallen. Studdert Kennedy will be seen to emphasise the latter when speaking to soldiers.

> For as it progressed the war acquired a logic and a momentum of its own. Their emotional investment in the Allied cause was reinforced by an investment steadily augmented in blood. The dead cried out to the living to finish the job and vindicate their sacrifice, although this meant adding untold millions to their number. No alternative remained. (Marrin 1974:222).

Where there might have been considerable theological conflict over the propriety of war considering the unprecedented numbers killed, there appears at the time to have been few if any chaplains who would risk 'peace mongering'. In World War I England had become too committed to war for army chaplains to preach peace in other than terms of spiritual harmony which would only be achieved between men and their God by the acceptance by all men of the Gospel and recognition by them of the unity of the human family in Christ; acceptably Christian without "rocking the boat".

Any society moulds the outlook of its members, and army chaplains in both World Wars were presented with a view of 'reality' which was in large measure a function of their social conditioning within the military. Anglican chaplains who represented the legally established faith of England felt a need to pay more regard to what the State was saying than perhaps did the dissenting churches and therefore it is unsurprising that their perception of the conflict was ambivalent as the threat to society was also a threat to the Established church. It must be added however that the temptation to use catastrophe to strengthen their own position in society was resisted neither by the Roman Catholics nor the Nonconformist churches. The former for so long stung by accusations of foreign loyalties was eager to prove its patriotism and the hierarchy did much to provide support for the war in the form of sufficient chaplains. The Nonconformists, who were equally keen to show the patriotism of a tradition long scorned, called upon the spirit of Cromwell and

Bunyan to bolster their own show of patriotism. Because both World Wars were seen by the political leaders as well as the majority of the population as just and necessary, opposition, especially by army chaplains, would have led to a dramatic lessening in their power and prestige. The complexity of social reality in war time regarding the pursuit of the war aims, beliefs and motivation is often over simplified, even to the extent of being presented in absolutist terms that "all the enemy does is evil and whatever we do is good."

The words and actions of the Reverend Studdert Kennedy will show the above tendency to adopt the popular propaganda and perceptions without fully testing them and to interpret them in a simplistic way representing them to his hearers in a manner which was acceptable without being challenging. The acceptance of the view that Germany or its rulers had become the agent of supernatural Evil led to the presentation of the Allies as agents of Good. Thus this-worldly concepts of just war, proportionality, legality and the restoration of rights, were replaced by a crusade expressed in other worldly terms where to die for one's country was sweet because opposition to Satan was Christlike. The transformation by Studdert Kennedy and other chaplains of the concept of a just war with limited objectives into the war of 'The Children of Light' for supernatural objectives was a position from which it was virtually impossible to retreat.

The organizational pressure both conscious and unconscious exerted by the Army upon individual chaplains constraining them to conform to military needs in preference to ecclesiastical goals has been compounded by the Chaplains' Department itself. If the Chaplaincy/Church in the Army saw itself as a Voluntary Associational Activity like scuba diving or bowling, those engaged in it would not be as likely to allow themselves to be influenced by the antipathy or prejudice of those who did not belong. It is because the Chaplains' Department is so concerned with the retention of the Army's favour that ever since the end of World War II there has been a readiness to play down the religious role of chaplaincy, other than in worship. This is not as bizarre as it might at first appear.

The tendency for organizations of all types to concentrate their energies or goals around activities that are easily quantified is markedly displayed by the Army Chaplains' Department. What is referred to is not the more predictable concentration on church attendance figures, but it is rather the significance bestowed upon the Army Church Centres, one at Bagshot in England and one at Lübbecke in Germany. The original role of such a centre, the first one set up at Bagshot in 1947, was to co-ordinate religious instruction in the British Army:

> first by establishing a Religious centre whose chief purpose it was asserted was to frame a clear authentic teaching for the Army and to get it first to the Chaplains and then to the troops (Hughes 1947)

In a chaplaincy-sponsored video entitled 'Seeking to Serve' 1990, aimed at showing the role of the Training Centres, is seen a staged interview between a Commanding Officer and the Chaplain Warden of Church House, Lübbecke. The Army Lieutenant Colonel surmises that perhaps there is 'more than a wee bit of Bible study involved in the courses' and asks whether this is true. The Chaplain Warden is at pains to soft pedal the religious input in courses, stating that there are an awful lot of false ideas about what Church House is for and continues: 'Now while we don't apologise for our Christian heritage or the Christian motivation behind our teaching, we certainly do not push religion down their throats.' One cannot help being reminded of what has been described as the stance of early Methodism before temporal authority as one of making the worst of both worlds. Like those Methodists, army chaplains end by serving as apologists for the Army in whose eyes they are increasingly marginalised and attempt to be no more than morale sustainers and a minor focus for social control, quite failing to fulfil their primary role: as religious professionals. That military phrase 'To shoot oneself in the foot' seems particularly apt as a synonym for such dysfunctional ministry, if ministry it is.

Role Perception

...chaplains as a group are increasingly uncertain about the proper modalities of their mission even as they are perhaps more keenly aware of their being the representatives of the transcendent amid the ugly contingencies of war and preparations therefor. The identity crisis of all ministers and priests cannot but affect ministers in uniform. Although some of them can retreat into bureaucratic paper work as administrative types, while a few can take personal satisfaction in being 'officers parentheses chaplains', many more are being drawn into being hyphenated ministers-officers but in the sense of being specialists in guidance counselling, drug addiction and other things besides worship and religious education at just about the moment when they had wrested for themselves an exclusively professional (ministerial) status throughout the services. (William 1971, 56)

The army chaplain as a minister of religion might be described as one who has attempted to internalise the Christian value system so that it gives an integrative cohesion to his total behaviour. It is the psychological and spiritual base which gives a person a rationale for behaving in one way rather than another, e.g. to oppose euthanasia rather than condone it. As for the majority of mankind so for an army chaplain, it is possible for him to be consciously aware of this inclination, but so much of his behaviour is tied in with the army milieu in which he finds himself and his activities so driven by existential considerations, that he might not allude to the spiritual dimension of his day to day behaviour.

There can be said to be two dimensions to the role of chaplains: that of minister of religion and that of membership of the military as an officer. He provides an ecclesiastical service to the military and he carries out his religious calling as clergyman as a member of the military. A worthwhile distinction can be made between the concept of 'role conflict' - the choice between two or more separate roles and 'role tension' - the strain between two dimensions of the same role.

8

Clergy at all times, and particularly in the context of this study, the clergy of the Church of England, have perceived themselves as the centre of an order of beliefs, values and symbols, which, while partaking of the nature of the sacred, gives English society its official religion. Sociologists have termed this, 'centricity', that is, to remain at the centre of society retaining an amount of power and prestige. It is conditional upon the Chaplains' Department allying itself to the prevailing values and interests of society. The Church of England has come to terms with the dual role of acting as the cement of British Society - the State religion - and preaching the Gospel. At times such as the Coronations of 1910, 1937 and 1953, the Church and the Monarchy take centre stage; at election times it is Parliament; in wartime it is the Armed Forces. The whole of society is interwoven with various interconnected subsystems which are linked through a shared authority and clearly perceived identity of interest. (Shils 1975:242) refers to this as a central value system which

> is constituted by the values which are pursued and affirmed by the élites. By their very possession of authority they attribute to themselves an essential affinity with the sacred elements of their society of which they regard themselves as custodians.

In both World Wars, but to a considerably lesser degree today, army chaplains shared in this close connection with what society has held to be sacred (not necessarily religious) and what was considered important by the élites of society. That share, ecclesiastical and military, enjoyed by army chaplains is twofold and is paradigmatic of the human need to be incorporated into something which can serve to transfigure individual existence. Chaplains in wartime are doubly important representatives of a temporarily superseded idea and agents of divine approval. It has been a contention of chaplains that one of their primary roles has been that of prophetic voice in the midst of war. Though there were individual clergymen both in the Church of England and other churches who were prepared to suffer the opprobrium resulting from opposition to the accepted wisdom and popular values, there is no record at any level of army chaplains publicly being among them. Though this is unsurprising it is incontrovertible that chaplains have a tendency to present themselves as outsiders while simultaneously belonging to and espousing the values, attitudes, outlook and often lifestyle of those at the centre, which in their case is that of a quite senior army officer. Chaplains are presented as specialists sent by churches and accepted by the military to perform very specific and limited service. That accepted simplistic view of their role one might believe would highlight the tension to be found between 'other worldly' behaviour recommended by Christianity and 'this-worldly' behaviour of engagement in war, which society at a particular time compels its members to adopt. In other words the tension would appear to be greatest in a war setting. The evidence seems incontrovertible except to chaplains themselves, that the chaplain, without directly encouraging more ardent participation in the war effort, is much more than a clergyman who happens to be an officer delegated to provide religious sustenance to those who are preparing for or taking part in war.

> Though there were some heroes and saints among the chaplains like Theodore Bayley Hardy, the typical chaplain of all denominations so often overdid 'his jolly implied disclaimers of any compromising connection with kingdoms not of this world. For one thing, he was, for the taste of people versed in carnage, a shade too fussily bloodthirsty.' (C.E. Montague) (Wilkinson, 1978, 117)

Such a belligerent attitude occasionally arose from an unlikely source:

> One of the Brigade Chaplains who shares our cellar defied his bishop, enlisted in the artillery and was a bombadier when he was reclaimed and transferred. To save his gold denture and best kit from roughing it down here, he left them in the Divisional Dump up north which the Germans have captured, all but ten lorry loads. Now he wants to kill Germans. (Dunn, 1994, 470)

10

It must be repeated that there is no question of attributing reprehensible behaviour to chaplains. Rather the findings point to examples of the phenomenon which has many names - reduction of cognitive dissonance, spontaneous rationalization or self-enforcing consistency. A psychologist Solomon E Asch conducted experiments where the subject in a rigged experiment finds, after initial consistency with the group that his/her judgements, for example judging the length of lines, conflict with the majority of the group whose members have been instructed to give false answers. The confused subject rather than remaining an 'outsider' will begin to adopt the 'view' of his peers. Peer pressure is not primarily an affliction besetting adolescents. Anyone who has worked inside a tight organization will admit how difficult it is to defy its grip especially by idealistic disloyalty. It can be modesty which gags, we might be wrong: we might not have the whole picture; we do not make the connections. Though the matter under discussion here need not be immoral and (though in the case of My Lai in Vietnam it was) chaplains become the victims of the greatest power to subvert; the power of friendship. (Purves 1992) exemplifies this from a 1945 novel by C S Lewis, *That Hideous Strength*, at the moment when a young man unsure of his acceptance by the inner ring is tasked by the laughing group round the fire to do something criminal

> There was no struggle, no sense of turning a corner.
> There may have been a time in the world's history
> when such moments fully revealed their gravity with
> witches prophesying on a blasted heath of visible
> Rubicons to be crossed. But for him it all slipped past
> in a chatter of laughter, of that intimate laughter
> between fellow professionals which of all earthly
> powers is strongest to make men do very bad things
> before they are yet, individually, very bad men.

It is worthy of note that in all the literature used for this research, with the exception of Zahn, no reference was found relating either to documented cases of breaches of the Geneva Convention by the British army or even to the potential role for chaplains in such an eventuality. That no such incidents happened is possible, but it

11

would appear to be more consistent with the theory of the subversive power of friendship, that if such an incident did occur, at best the chaplain would either be unaware or prepared to give 'his side' the benefit of the doubt, or at worst avoid altogether confronting army colleagues.

The assertion of Muttram (1991) in his research on Chaplaincies that interviews with Chaplains made it clear that there was no tension between responsibility to the parent church and the organization to which the chaplain was appointed, can only stand if most organizational research is ignored. He then concedes that point but in very imprecise terms

> While it may be true that 'who pays the piper calls the tune' a common factor in all employing organizations is that in the case of chaplains, this dual accountability is more or less formally recognised (Muttram 1991:103)

There is a marked reluctance on the part of chaplains to accept what in almost any other role would be self-evidently obvious viz. Zahn's contention (1969:32) that

> the military chaplain..... lives and breathes the military life to the extent that his actions will, for the most part assume a military coloration.

In preference to using hypothetical wrongdoing, a better example is given by a Vietnam wartime incident. It was asserted that the United States Military Vicar, Cardinal Cooke's Pastoral Message of Peace - May 1972, was given to all priests. "No one impeded priests in the forces from disseminating the pastoral." (O'Connor 1982:74) Psychologists and Sociologists would reply that the question was not whether military chaplains were free to pass on the message but that they would be much less likely to do so by reason of their incorporation into the Military, their loyalty to it and to the audience they would address. It must be reiterated that the integrity of chaplains is not being questioned. It is precisely because they are as other men are, that their very membership is prone to prejudice them against opposition to authority.

12

Consider the August 1965 incident at Cam Ne filmed by Morley Safer of CBS News. As Vietnamese women with terrified children clutching at their skirts wailed in the foreground, US Marines, Zippo lighters in hand, burned their homes to the ground. Whatever minuscule tactical advantage was gained by that action was totally overshadowed by the enormous strategic damage it inflicted on American public support. Burning defenceless women and children out of house and home wasn't some thing Americans should be doing. Those were the kind of things the bad guys did.

Where was that unit's chaplain while this was going on? Did he question the morality of the operation? And if he did, did the commander listen? These are the same questions that arise again almost three years later during the running amok elements of the 1st Battalion, 20th Infantry at My Lai in March 1968.

The worst atrocity in the entire history of the U.S. Army, its litany of rape, sodomy and cold-blooded murder was even worse than was portrayed in the press. Where were the Battalion, Brigade and American Division chaplains when the atrocities were taking place? Where were they during the next year while the atrocities were being covered up? What kind of moral climate had they created, or failed to create, that would allow such a thing to happen? Those are hard questions, questions that have not gone away with the end of the Vietnam war. (Summers, 1990, 7)

When Churches - and chaplains recruited from them - fail to warn that there is no compelling reason to take the hugely significant initial step of getting into a war, it should come as no surprise that they failed to restrain the means by which the war was waged. This problem and the real failure to come to terms with it according to Zahn, could scarcely be given better illustration than the quotation attributed to Fr Daniel Byrne, US Army Republic of Vietnam Deputy Command Chaplain: "We do not debate the morality of the war in general or the morality of any particular war. Our job is to look after the spiritual welfare of the men." (Cox, 1971, 85) Like Moses or

Jeremiah a chaplain longs to belong. Confronting the Pharaoh or the Commanding Officer, particularly in wartime, virtually guarantees ostracism. More likely was what Major General Sir William Thwaites described, when he asked for a more bellicose sermon in 1917

> On that Sunday I got hold by accident of a blushing young curate straight out from England - but he preached the most bloodthirsty sermon I had ever listened to (Wilkinson 1978:152)

Not only was the chaplain being controlled but his sermon was an exercise in social control of his congregation. It would not have been impossible for the chaplain to refuse to 'toe the line' but, in the context of the coercion and control exercised in any compact group, we see an example both of the mechanism of control and a very powerful one. The chaplain reduced any feelings of deviance by getting rid of the psychological tension in his bellicose sermon. The main way of reducing dissonance is by adding consonant cognitions and changing dissonant cognitions and, if Freedman and Sears (1981:405) are correct, the following is an overview of how it might work in the case of a minister who joins the army. He possibly finds it difficult to convince himself that pacifism or joining the army is unimportant. He may then decide that joining the army is a ministry to a special group, a belief which is consonant with joining and thus reduces some dissonance. Esteem, status, rank and pay, all of which will benefit his wife and family, are also good reasons for joining. If dissonance is still felt, gradual jettisoning of the belief in pacifism as 'unrealistic' and adoption of a pragmatic view of national defence further reduces cognitive dissonance. '*Si vis pacem, para bellum*' is not an unreasonable motto. Chaplains like others are influenced by experience while engaging in discrepant behaviour.

Accountability

It will be shown that chaplains are given authority within the army to exercise the functions of their calling. Examples indicate that the parameters of their duties and responsibilities have been expressed in very broad terms. This could be construed as an appreciation by the Chaplains' Department of the breadth of church ministry permitting the freedom in the furtherance of that ministry. The evidence would seem to suggest something other, viz. that nobody within the Chaplains' Department, from successive Chaplains General down, has been able to state unequivocally what constitutes ministry in general nor military chaplaincy in particular. Each minister of religion coming to the army from his own denominational background is prepared to relinquish a certain amount of freedom in return for position (officer status) and reward (substantial remuneration) but not to the extent of being told what the details of his ministry should be. It is to a very large degree presumed, as the Chaplains' Handbook bears out, that the ministers know their own ministry and need little or no instruction how to execute it in the army environment. It might be expected that in the highly regulated hierarchical organization called the army, considerably closer control would be exercised over chaplains both by the army itself and by the Chaplains' Department in particular, than might be the case in civilian ministries. The reality is that the control is remarkably loose. Of course the Chaplains' Department is in control of recruitment, retention and deployment of chaplains. A chaplain is given responsibilities over very specific areas - areas or units rather than churches, and it is assumed that he will carry out his duties to the best of his ability in accordance with the directions, procedures and policies as indicated in the Handbook. The organizational goal is that the individual chaplain fulfils the role of minister to that community to which he is sent; in light of the above, an objective left deliberately vague.

The amount of autonomy exercised by each chaplain is almost total. Though on the level of formal organizational authority, a chaplain is governed by successive levels of formation commands:- Regiment, Garrison, Brigade, Division, Corps, Army Headquarters, each chaplain has little or no control over the ministerial activities of the newer chaplains within his command except, as will be seen, when a chaplain's behaviour gravely upsets the smooth running of the system or where there are disciplinary reasons for moving him. Such moves are rare.

Controls however are exercised, the most influential being that written by his superiors upon a chaplain, known as an Annual Confidential Report. Even this, which is intended to judge the quality of an individual chaplain's performance and determine his value to the organization, is heavily trait-based and scored on a four point scale. Trait assessment is not only notoriously difficult to quantify (how loyal is very loyal?) but unlike for instance assessments of productivity in the car industry, is extremely subjective. Other than in the exercise of his core role, where as members of his congregation they might judge him, the interaction between the chaplain and those responsible for assessing him formally can be very slight. It is therefore in each chaplain's interest not only to appear to work hard but be seen to do so by those significant individuals who will report on him. It is in the chaplain's interest to cultivate the friendship of those who will report on him or those who will be consulted by those who write the report. So long as he submits the required paperwork demanded by the higher Chaplaincy formation, conducts his Church services to the satisfaction of his congregation and retains as high a visibility profile as possible, what the chaplain does with his time is almost entirely at his own discretion. The following quotation from a letter sent by the Assistant Chaplain General to all his chaplains in Germany in 1991, and quoted with his permission, clearly illustrates many of the points just made. The underlying threat will not be missed:

> I am aware of the work-load placed on chaplains. I am also aware that fewer Padre's Hours than ever before are being held. Perhaps each chaplain should reappraise his ministry and try to order it in a more effective manner. The formal planning of Padre's Hours may need looking into by Brigade/Garrison Senior Chaplains who could act as trainees to the newly

arrived for whom army ministry is something completely new. I would add that having a Quarterly Reporting System is of inestimable benefit to Divisional Senior Chaplains as they assess the performance (or lack of it) when preparing Confidential Reports or considering extensions to Short Service Commissions etc. Having seen the word 'none' repeated so very often, I do wonder what some chaplains at Unit level are in fact doing.

Commitment

"Commitment can be considered to be composed of three elements: satisfaction, identification and involvement" (Hodge & Anthony 1988:431).

The very high degree of *satisfaction* expressed by chaplains cannot be divorced from very real but subtle influences of which the majority of chaplains are unaware or have so absorbed into their world view that they no longer notice them. A minister of religion of whatever persuasion knows that he is an army chaplain but does not necessarily realise the manifold subtle and profound ways in which his commitment has shaped and continues to shape the manner he perceives life. Berger expressed it vividly when he said that ideologies do not operate in front of our faces but from behind our backs.

Identification and *involvement* is brought about most acutely by the wearing of army uniform and in the case of a chaplain a very real pride in the fact that it is an officer's uniform. The social status of ministers of religion has fallen steadily since the beginning of the century but the clergyman turned chaplain is transformed from being a relatively insignificant individual in one sphere, to becoming in his army chaplaincy a significant member of another, so it should be unsurprising that he will think highly of a community in which he is given significance. Membership therefore of the Royal Army Chaplains' Department gives him a significance within the Army and a restoration of prestige largely lacking outside the Services. It might be added that without the status given to chaplains by rank, the prestige would be denied by the Army.

In World War I and even in World War II the church's place in society and therefore the army chaplain's place was accepted and understood. More and more people now regard the chaplain as an anachronism, representing a church whose role and function are far from clear. The church's alliance with the army continues to give its ministers a spurious appearance of authority and strength. By its association with an organization which continues to have authority and legitimacy, the chaplain within the army is given an appearance of significance which his civilian counterpart has lost in the lives of the overwhelming majority of the contemporary population of Britain.

There is a close congruence between the personal goals of chaplains and the goals of the army with the result that there is a high degree of *satisfaction* in the perception that the relationship is mutually beneficial. As well as the perceived advantages previously related, perhaps the greatest attraction is that the chaplain can still see himself in his own image of his role as that of an independent professional man, even though it is often only in the area of ritual - the solemnization of significant events in army life - that the chaplain is perceived to have 'expert power'. It should be mentioned in association with the claim to professionalism that the army chaplain has distinctive dress plus rank at all times. Even though the authority and legitimacy which a profession derives from its possession of a knowledge or skill which society deems important has greatly shrunk the case of the clergy, it is still possible for army chaplains to believe they possess readily recognizable skills like doctors, dentists or vets, when the truth is that

> Beyond their liturgical functions the clergy find it particularly difficult to make statements about the content of their role in terms to which the rest of society can readily relate (Anthony, 1984:282)

Chaplains' membership of an elite is much more obvious, though once more it is about their officer status that chaplains show ambivalence. If role is defined as a named social position characterised by a set of personal qualities and activities determined by those involved in the situation, evaluation is assisted at a microsociological level where each individual chaplain interacts with others through his social role. What is surely unique is that the chaplain's fulfilment of his religious calling as clergyman is military. The chaplain, while often attempting to play down his officer status, is forced to admit that the exercise of his role without it would be made more difficult. It should be interjected here that the lack of badges of rank, much vaunted by Royal Naval chaplains, is something of a red herring. Royal Naval chaplains' accommodation, conditions of service, seniority and pay scales are those of officers not other-ranks. They eat in the Wardroom - open only to officers - and are treated by all naval personnel as officers, in every respect comparable to their army counterparts. Though insignia of rank may be lacking to Naval chaplains, 'Where two or three are gathered together, one of them is senior' or as Shakespeare put it, 'A rose by any other name would smell as sweet.'

As the Reverend Creighton was so acutely aware in World War I, chaplains were officers in the full sense of the word and separated from the men by a social chasm, not only by reason of their clerical status, but widened by their officer status. There is no doubt, as anyone has found who has taken the trouble as I have, to interview non-officers on the subject, that the men see the chaplain's rank in the context of the total military structure in which soldiers reside in the lower echelons, and consciously or unconsciously see the chaplain in the upper echelons as 'one of them'. A particular anxiety of chaplains is fed by anything which might interfere with their total acceptance as members of the military community. Identification with those to whom he ministers is repeatedly proposed as an advantage so that uniform becomes the litmus test for this alliance. Yet closer observation would seem to indicate that the chaplain would prefer to reject symbolic identification with their clerical status lest it interfere with total acceptance within the military. The tension is well summed up by stating that it is insufficient to say that everyone, officers, men and certainly the chaplain recognises his rank as something other than what it purports to be. On the contrary if the chaplain wants to be taken seriously in his spiritual aspect, it will not help to present him in a manner which suggests he is **really** not what he appears to be. (Zahn 1969:290)

Evangelist and/or Propagandist

Though a formal member of the Army organization which employs and pays him, there are numerous examples of reluctance on the part of those to whom the chaplain was sent to accept him on his own terms. Doctors or dentists, especially in wartime, were encouraged to carry out their professional role without any expectation that they would engage in other activities. Though his specifically religious duties could scarcely be ignored, the value of a chaplain was often measured principally by *what else* he could do over and above his ill-defined core role. Army chaplains have frequently been guilty of belittling, albeit indirectly, their own religious ministry. It was by laying claim to a practical primary role, asserted one chaplain, that he assured his inclusion in the first 'wave' on D Day both in the invasion of Sicily and Normandy. "To justify my place I always had myself assigned a definitely medical role." (Hughes 1944b:10). The imprecision of the chaplain's role time and again drove him to seek to do something useful, which often resulted in a greater pride being taken in that achievement than any connected with his religious ministry. Tea made by the Catering Corps remained tea; tea made by the chaplain was transubstantiated into Christian witness and pious endeavour. It has been suggested that because the activity of a priest or minister had no visible effect, unlike the ministrations of doctors or dentists, chaplains had a psychological need to prove that they were 'worth their salt' by making a perceptible contribution.

In the theatre of war opportunities for pastoral work are restricted and a chaplain in battle possesses no recognizable skills. One particular role of a chaplain is to reduce the tension between the Christian conviction that every man is my brother, and the army's

20

operational necessity to kill or neutralize as many of the enemy as possible. One chaplain (Lloyd, 1950:64) attempted to spell out such a task in a way that would appear to have neither the support of Law nor Christianity.

> If you fire a rifle or pull a gun-lanyard or release a bomb lever you are not responsible for the deaths caused. The responsibility lies on the nation as a whole. Perhaps I should qualify that remark. You are a citizen of the nation and so you share in the responsibility. You are no more responsible than anyone else. In the Forces the actual firer of a lethal weapon is no more responsible for the death it produces than the man who brings the rations or keeps the records. Of course that only applies to actions authorized by the State for the purpose of winning the war.

It seems incontrovertible that if the duties of a chaplain were no more than holding religious services, providing the sacraments and preaching in very general terms, a pacifist could fulfil those duties. The manifest functions of chaplaincy was to provide for the spiritual needs of the Army. Its latent function has always been to give legitimation to the enterprise by the association of Throne and Altar. Sociologically speaking, specialists in the army are there because their contribution has a beneficial effect on the overall military effort. Consideration of the contrary only reinforces that truth. By upholding the values, tradition and discipline of the army whose duty it is to protect the *status quo*, the instrumental value of religion and the specific role of the chaplain can be most clearly perceived.

The close identification of Church and State in England which was the result of a political solution to a religious problem has resulted in almost unquestioning acceptance by the Church of the decision of the government of the day, or the consecration of the national cause whether it was right or wrong. In 1902 the rhetorical question was asked: 'where have the priests ever failed to bless a war supported by authority and popular passion?' Part explanation of the reason concerns the nature of Anglicanism, which due to its legal position within the State, is denied the possibility of having a theological doctrine separating the faithful from a corrupting world. Citizenship implied church membership bringing with them civic duties. The onus of reminding citizens of the obligation to rally to the defence of the country fell heavily upon the clergy and those who best supported the military effort were those most closely identified with it - the military chaplains. It became virtually impossible for army chaplains to exercise any prophetic role for each had his own interests to preserve as well as a material and emotional investment in the society he inhabited. The Church in general and army chaplains in particular have not opposed wars which the rest of society deemed just and necessary, for to have done so would have resulted in diminished power and prestige if not organizational demise. It was by ecclesiastical support of the State that led individual clergymen to accompany units of the national army into battle. Organizational demands have structured army chaplaincy in ways that are mutually beneficial but with the self-evident premise that if the army did not consider it an advantage to have a chaplaincy or a particular chaplain it would dispense with their services. The formation of the link between army and church and its operational consequences will now be progressively considered.

Chapter 2

Organizational Structure of British Army Chaplaincy

Early History

Dearly beloved brethren, the Scriptures say, will those Hussars stop shuffling, 'I heard a voice from heaven saying,' Fifth Dragoon Guards stop rattling those scabbards!

(From a 19th century sermon)

The Reverend Father Brown, a Roman Catholic Chaplain during the defence of Kabul in 1879 when things were about at their worst, went round the hospitals exhorting all who could possibly turn out, to do so and get hold of a rifle; "It's Jesus Christ against Mahomet," he said, "and we're sure to win."

The tradition of a specially appointed holy man accompanying soldiers into battle is mentioned in Deuteronomy 20 : 2-4;

When you are about to join battle, the priest must come forward and address the people. He must say to them 'Listen, Israel, you are about to join battle with your enemies. Do not be faint hearted. Let there be no fear or trembling or alarm as you face them. Yahweh your God is marching with you to fight your enemies for you and to make you victorious'.

What is remarkable is how subsequent Christian military chaplains have in their exhortations to soldiers before battle so closely echoed these sentiments with their appeal to raise morale and their assurance, real or imagined, that God was on their side. Protection did not always extend to such priests as is shown in 1 Samuel 4:11

where the two priest sons of Eli, Hophni and Phinehas were killed when the Philistines captured the Ark of the Covenant - the earliest evidence of chaplain fatalities.

In the Christian era Constantine, who legalized Christianity in 313 and adopted the cross as a battle standard, established the earliest known formal connection between Christianity and the military. That clergy took part in battles as combatants is known from the Venerable Bede's History of the English Church and People written in 731, and that they were not chaplains in the modern sense, but fully combatant participants can be gathered from the prohibition of the Council of Ratisbon 742 banning -

> the servant of God in every way from bearing arms or fighting in the Army.... except those alone who because of the sacred office, namely for celebrating of Mass and caring for the relics of the Saints, have been designated for this office.

The Synod of Westminster 1175 prohibited the clergy from taking up arms or going about in armour, indication enough that earlier rules often went unheeded even by Bishops, one of whom, Anthony de Beck, Bishop of Durham, in full armour led the charges of the English knights against the Scottish pikemen in the Battle of Falkirk 1298.

Individual regiments which were in effect the self contained active units of the British Army, had a chaplain on their staff, as is shown from an Elizabethan army standing order placing a Preacher or Chaplain alongside the Surgeon, Quartermaster and Provost Marshal (1558-1603). The provision of such a chaplain was incumbent upon the colonels commanding, who took this responsibility seriously, at least until the beginning of the 18th Century. Cromwell's New Model Army, more serious still, continued the practice of the appointment of a chaplain to a regiment either by the commander or chosen by the unit.

As commissioned Field Officers who received pay, regimental chaplains, like many of their contemporary civilian clergymen, were absentee chaplains engaging others in their stead for poorer pay and by 1793 the system neared collapse when only one regimental chaplain was present for duty with an entire Corps. An example of a state of affairs which led to the reorganisation of the chaplaincy system is provided by Duncan Wright, one of Wesley's preachers, who had himself been a soldier. Watkins (1906:8) wrote:

> Were the Chaplains men of real piety and courage much might be done in the Army, but the Chaplaincy is generally a kind of sinecure and the care of souls is left to any worthless wretch that will do it at an easy rate. When we lay in one City, the care of four or five regiments was left to an unhappy man, who was an object of common ridicule among the soldiers for his perpetual drunkeness.

The Army Chaplains' Department

By the Royal Warrant of September 23 1796 the system was abolished and in its place was established an organized Chaplains' Department. This had become increasingly necessary in the light of the British Army's experience in fighting the French in the North American continent as well as in the War of American Independence. Chaplains to the Army were henceforth seen as an integral part of it and were recruited and paid as such. What is notable is an abiding definition of the work of chaplains, by both the British and the Americans as 'cura animarum', the 'care of souls'; to preach, to pray, to administer the sacraments, to minister to the sick and bury the dead. In its present form, the Royal Army Chaplains' Department (RAChD) perceives itself as the direct heir to the reforms introduced in 1796.

Denominational Growth

Unremarkably following the religious Reformation, official chaplains belonged to the Church of England but some Scottish regiments which were Presbyterian appointed their own chaplains. Presbyterian ministers were first recognised by the War Office as official chaplains in 1827 and Roman Catholic priests obtained the same recognition in 1836, though they had to wait until 1858 to receive payment. The Methodists, or Wesleyans as they were known, had a longer fight for religious freedom in the Army. In July 1839 General Lord Hill, the Commander-in-Chief, issued a 'General Order' giving to the soldiers full liberty to attend the Worship of Almighty God according to the forms prescribed by his own religion, but this was largely ignored at local level at the instigation of serving Church of England Chaplains. The Crimean War 1854-5 saw the first Wesleyan minister sent on active service though still only with the status of camp follower. To a Roman Catholic who might have believed only those of his persuasion were discriminated against by the Church of England, the following quotation from Watkins (1906:88) has a familiar ring

> But whenever the Chaplain General could quote an unrepealed regulation or order that was to the disadvantage of the Methodists, he did so and then Mr Herbert, the Secretary of State for War, was powerless to assist.

Under the title 'Other Protestants', Wesleyan ministers from and after April 1st 1881 were put on a par with officiating Chaplains of the Church of England, Roman Catholic and Presbyterian denominations, though the first time a commission was granted to a Methodist minister in the Regular Army is reported in the London Gazette November 12, 1900. It is worth noting that only in 1889 were Jews recognised as a separate denomination and in 1920 the distinction between Church of England, Presbyterian, Wesleyan and United Board was formally acknowledged.

Leadership Structure

Though there was a position, even before the Cromwellian Commonwealth, known as Chaplain General, that title merely reflected the assignment on the Commander-in-Chief's staff or that of the King, without conferring on the holder any supervisory powers over other Chaplains. This changed in 1796 when the newly appointed Chaplain General became a Departmental Head with responsibility for the administration of Chaplains, and thus it has remained with minor modifications ever since.

The most senior chaplain in the British Army is the Chaplain General (CG) ranking as a Major General who is appointed by the Army Board and has the status of a Director of Service at the Ministry of Defence, Army, MOD (A). Until the appointment of the The Reverend James Harkness on 1st January 1987, the accepted view was that expressed by an Anglican Chaplain, Middleton Brumwell (1943:32):

> It is an unwritten principle that whilst the Church of England remains the State Church of the realm, the Chaplain General shall be a priest of the Church of England. The Deputy Chaplain General (DCG) must either be a Presbyterian or Methodist or United Board.

One premise of this principle was the majority membership in the Army of those professing to belong to the Church of England. The other was the natural justice of the most senior appointment being held by a minister of the Church of England, which provided and provides a substantial majority of the total number of chaplains at any one time. To illustrate denominational breakdown: In the First World War the number of chaplains rose from 117 at the outbreak of war, to 3475 by November 1918. Of these 1985 were Church of England (57.1%), 649 Roman Catholic (18.7%), 303 Presbyterian (8.7%), 256 Wesleyan (7.4%), 251 United Board [Baptist, Congregational, Primitive Methodist and United Methodist] (7.2%), 16 Jewish (0.5%), 10 Welsh Calvinist (0.3%) and 5 Salvationists (0.1%). The total number of chaplains serving in 1990 was 156 of whom 100 Church of England (64.1%), includes 11 Church of Ireland and 4 Church of Wales, 22 Catholic (14.1%), 16 Church of Scotland (10.3%), 10 Methodist (6.4%), 8 United Board (5.1%).

The Chaplain General

On the retirement of The Venerable Archdeacon Frank Johnson in 1986, past precedent was overturned by the appointment by the Army Board of The Reverend James Harkness, a Minister of the

27

Church of Scotland, significantly also an Established Church. Few if any questioned James Harkness's competence - he was after all the Deputy Chaplain General - but considerable misgivings were expressed over the appointment, by the Church of England establishment both inside and outside the army, who criticised what they saw as an encroachment upon a tried and tested, equitable historical practice.

It was reported that the Bishop of the Forces addressed a meeting of Church of England chaplains and stated that the appointment of the Reverend Harkness should be opposed at every turn, for, unless some protests were registered 'they would be offering the appointment to Roman Catholics next!' Though the appointment of a non-Anglican Chaplain General was unimaginable to many British Anglican chaplains, the appointment as Chaplain General, of chaplains of various denominations, has proved workable as instanced by the United States Army from 1920 until 1980 where there has been 13 Chiefs of Chaplains, 4 Baptists, 1 Southern Baptist, 3 Roman Catholic, 1 Congregationalist, 1 Episcopalian, 1 Lutheran and 2 Methodists. Of course the United States does not have a state religion.

As the office of Chaplain General is administrative and impinges only peripherally on the day to day lives of chaplains, the change in leadership has made no significant difference to how the Chaplains' Department is run. (Incidentally, Dr. Victor Dobbin, an Irish Presbyterian, succeeded James Harkness as Chaplain General in 1995.) To add more international focus to that British Army policy change of leadership, in World War 1 a 62 year old Methodist chaplain, John Alfred Luxford, was appointed Senior Chaplain to the New Zealand Forces, but his appointment was made without the consent of the three major denominations, particularly of the Church of England, so on their objection, a lay Brigadier was appointed in his place. He called together the Senior Chaplains of the four major denominations and with them drew up a workable system which survived the war. Mindful of the trouble over that appointment of a non-Church of England Senior Chaplain, in the Second World War the New Zealand Army Board sounded out the Churches in New

Zealand first, but there was no objection to the appointment of a Presbyterian, James William McKenzie, as Senior Chaplain.

Successive Church of England Chaplain Generals had been assisted by a Deputy Chaplain General ranking as Brigadier, who was either Church of Scotland, Methodist or United Board. It should be noted at this point that Roman Catholic priests, ever since their admission into the Army as paid chaplains in 1858, initially, and since, have reported directly to the War Office as it was then known, and not to the Chaplain General, to whom all other chaplains reported. The reason for this was that Roman Catholics, so long discriminated against by the State as well as by the Established Church, considered that they would be more equitably treated by relating directly to the Army Board rather than through the Anglican Chaplain General. Under the Adjutant General, who has overall responsibility for the army administration of the whole RAChD, the Principal Catholic Chaplain, ranking as a Full Colonel, administers all Roman Catholic chaplains. All matters of ecclesiastical concern are referred to the appropriate church authority by the 2nd Permanent Under Secretary of State who is the contact within the Ministry of Defence for the participating churches. As a consequence of the Roman Catholic chaplains constituting a semi-autonomous group within the Chaplains' Department, their chaplains are not considered for the post either of Chaplain General or Deputy Chaplain General, who are appointed by the Army Board from members of the non-Roman Catholics, known as the Unified Department. In a country where it is still forbidden for either the Sovereign or the Prime Minister to be a Roman Catholic, though not a logical necessity it is not surprising that a Roman Catholic is also forbidden the leadership of chaplaincy in the Army. It must be emphasized however that relations between the Unified Branch and Roman Catholic chaplains have improved markedly over the past thirty years, so that there is no fundamental reason why the Roman Catholics should not belong to a unified army chaplaincy, thereby enhancing manpower resources to provide chaplaincy for a greater number of soldiers rather than a parochial ministry to a small group of co-religionists.

The Free Church Denominations constituted a United Board in 1914 acting together in securing the appointment of chaplains of these denominations and watching over their rights and interests in the armed forces. When in 1932 the various Methodist groups amalgamated and legally became the Methodist Church, the United Navy, Army and Air Force Board was reconstituted and became responsible for Baptist and Congregationalist personnel. Since 1972 the Board consists of the Baptist Union, the United Reform Church and the Congregationalist Federation.

The Chaplain General was responsible on the military side for the administration of everything affecting the moral and spiritual welfare of the Land Forces of the Crown - for all denominations other than Roman Catholics. On the ecclesiastical side the Chaplain General's jurisdiction was given him by special commission of the Archbishops of Canterbury and York, which charged him with the spiritual supervision and direction of the Chaplains of Her Majesty's Land Forces and the general superintendence of the work of the Church of England among the officers and men of Her Majesty's army.

On the appointment of a minister of the Church of Scotland as Chaplain General equity was upheld by making a Church of England chaplain the Deputy Chaplain General. He was eventually given the title the Venerable Archdeacon, formerly given to Church of England Chaplains General, as the senior Church of England chaplain delegated by the Bishop to the Forces with the care of Church of England clergy. This title enabled him to retain Army Chaplaincy representation on the Synod of the Church of England, lost with the appointment of a non-Anglican Chaplain General. The exceptional nature of James Harkness's appointment is best highlighted by the denominational representation at the top of the Chaplains' Department, which reflects overall representation. Six out of nine chaplains ranking as Colonel belong to the Church of England.

The method by which a chaplain reaches such senior appointment in the Chaplains' Department is made as with other Army Officers, by being promoted and such promotion is made through an Army Board Selection process. The basis upon which the Board makes its recommendation is provided by Annual Confidential Reports which are made each year upon all chaplains. As there is input into the Report by both Senior Chaplains and Senior Army

Officers, there is often consultation between those who assess a chaplain before anything is written. In this way consensus may be reached and potentially divergent assessments made to converge. What is obvious is that the army, in the person of senior officers, has a view of chaplains and it is to that view that we now turn.

Chaplains' Status Within the Army

> Father, Mother and Me,
> Sister and Auntie say;
> All the peole like us are We,
> And everyone else is They.
>
> All good people agree,
> And all good people say;
> All nice people, like Us, are We,
> And everyone else is They.

Rudyard Kipling

The fact that chaplains are officially appointed by the Secretary of State for Defence makes clear that they are employees of the Army. Though nominated by the accredited representatives of the various Churches and denominations, the overall responsibility for the administration of the Chaplains' Department rests with the Adjutant General and under him the Chaplain General and the Principal Catholic Chaplain.

The newly appointed chaplain, like any other officer, is given a number in sequence with line officers and the Ministry of Defence Chaplains (Army) arranges for his commissioning, and the date of his appointment is published in the Supplement to the London Gazette. He is granted a Short Service Commission lasting three years, which is deemed sufficient time for the minister to learn what chaplaincy in the Army entails, with adequate security of tenure to make a considered judgement whether he wishes to extend beyond that period, and for the Chaplains' Department to judge whether he possesses those attributes considered necessary to fulfil the role of military chaplain.

Within the military establishment certain attitudes have altered less radically than has been the case in society as a whole. Though there have been times when an anti-chaplain movement was strong - this was particularly so in the United Kingdom following the First World War - the military establishment has managed to retain a strict hierarchical structure which has been eroded to a large degree in British society, and will still acknowledge a role for the chaplain without being too clear as to what that is.

All chaplains are officers in a profession which can be seen as more than an organization; rather a complete style of life. Each officer alongside the chaplain is a member of a community which makes calls on the individual over and above so-called work time. Of course this is not unique to the military; doctors, nurses and the police would make similar claims, but as a member of the military establishment, the chaplain is assured of essential acceptance and takes his place in the upper echelons of a strictly hierarchical organization. However many attempts are made to play down his officer status by chaplains themselves or by apologetes for chaplains, this remains the barrier which separates 'Them' from 'Us'.

The Queen's Commission

At the risk of labouring the point, the distinction between those who are granted the Queen's Commission, (commissioned officers), and those who are not, is crucial to an understanding of the position and status of chaplains within the military. The British Army is a constitutional army. Parliament gives consent to the maintenance of a standing army by passing the Army Act each year. Without this parliamentary action, the army would legally cease to exist. The government of the army, however, is vested in the Crown. Hence the regulations for its administration are entitled "The Queen's Regulations"; its serving members are paid in accordance with the 'Pay Warrant'. Commissioned officers hold the 'Queen's Commission'. The enlistment of a soldier in contrast is a contract between the Sovereign and the soldier - the old phrase 'to take the Queen's shilling' as a synonym for enlistment, serves to highlight the nature of the contract.

Ministers of religion are commissioned as chaplains, placed among the higher echelons of a strictly rank-ordered society, entering nine ranks above a private soldier and only eight below a Field Marshal. The tension most commonly felt by the chaplains is not that of reconciling the Christian exhortation of turning the other cheek and loving one's enemies with massive retaliation and surgical air strikes, but on the very personal and human level of consorting sufficiently with the soldiery so as to have it noticed and favourably commented upon by the soldiers themselves, without losing that link with his peers i.e. fellow officers, which is so necessary for success. Many chaplains attempt to deny this but that would appear to entail a denial, patently false, that the vast majority of army chaplains adopt the manners, dress, general social behaviour and lifestyle of their fellow officers than that of those who are not officers. Becoming more a 'soldiers' chaplain' than an 'officers' chaplain' is the army equivalent of the colonial experience of 'going native'. It is promotional suicide. Anthony Russell (1984:33) maintained that

> A clergyman of the last quarter of the eighteenth century ..... could partake in the interests and recreations of the gentry to a degree that made it difficult for contemporaries to regard the clergy as a distinct body.

The experience of officers, senior non-commissioned officers and servicemen and women is that a chaplain, within living memory and beyond, partakes in the interests, recreations and demeanour of his fellow officers to such a degree that makes it difficult for them to regard the chaplain as anything but another officer. In so far as he impinges upon their lives at all, he embarks upon a sort of tightrope walk upon which he will be expected to be at ease with his fellow officers while trying not to ignore, as much as they do him, those who are not officers. It is now an undeniable fact and the universal experience of army chaplains, that for the greater part of their ministry they will have disproportionately more contact, ecclesiastically, administratively and socially with fellow officers than they will with non-commissioned ranks. It should not be altogether surprising, that in a closely rank-ordered society, which to a large degree has disappeared in Britain as a whole, the chaplain conforms to the role expectation demanded of him by his officer status and rank. The accommodation given to him as an officer means that all his immediate neighbours are only those of officer status and thus it is not surprising that he naturally becomes friendly with those of a similar status. If it is less true now than ten to twenty years ago, that the bulk of his small congregation would be drawn from the families of married officers, it is still true particularly for a Church of England Chaplain, that the help and support he receives is still disproportionately given by this group.

On Easter Sunday 1918 Oswin Creighton noted that a number of officers attended the Eucharist services he had arranged but hardly any men

> The war is really breaking no barriers down. The hardest line ever drawn in human society is that between officers and men. Do what you will, you cannot destroy or even lessen it .... they live in two different worlds, and the chaplain lives in the officers' world. (Wilkinson 1978:46)

It cannot be too strongly stated that those who assert that the carrying of officer rank, in the case of Army and RAF chaplains and the status of officer in the case of Naval chaplains, is of little or no consequence, are doing so in the face of the overwhelming evidence of those psychological, sociological and organizational studies in this field.

The Queen's Regulations

The Queen's Regulations regarding religion and the Chaplaincy Services begin by stating that "chaplains are commissioned by Her Majesty the Queen to provide spiritual well-being of service personnel and their families." To achieve that provision it is recommended that chaplains are to be given every assistance to fulfil their ministry for the stated reason that "the reverent observance of religion in the armed forces is of the highest importance." These army regulations might come as a considerable surprise to many who might have believed that religion and the military either should not or do not mix. In fact the link between the British Army and the Church has never really been broken. At the end of the eighteenth century when the traffic in chaplaincies became so scandalous, concern not indifference prompted the issuing of the Warrant, (Chaplains' Department Journal 1930:292), that

> no sale, exchange or transfer of commissions by the present chaplains should be permitted after the 25th December 1796 unless the application for that purpose should have been previously made: and in this interval that no chaplaincy should be sold for more than was given for it, nor should the purchaser have any claim to sell the same again.

Such a Warrant acknowledged the corruption and endeavoured to stop it, and was engendered by the moral, spiritual and social awakening in which John Wesley and his followers played a considerable part. It is long since Parliament legislated for the people at large compelling religious observance, but by Queen's Regulations 'Commanding Officers are to encourage religious observance by those under their command and are themselves to set a good example in this respect.' They are also

> to ensure that chaplains and officiating chaplains are at all times treated with the respect due to their calling and given every facility for the efficient performance of their duty. Chaplains should be addressed both officially and otherwise by their ecclesiastical title or official appointment and not by their relative rank or military title.

The final sentence of Queen's Regulations 5.275 touches on the subject of rank and status that Commissioned chaplains are, however, entitled to the compliments which are due to an officer of the same relative rank.

35

Two of the notable features of the Queen's Regulations relating to chaplains are their brevity and their non-sectarian tone. Where distinctions are made, they are done so to uphold the rights and specify the duties of the chaplains to the various religious groups and not to accentuate differences, still less to create them. Zahn (1971:78) confirms this but with a different emphasis stating that what concerns the Services is the efficiency of performance of the priestly and pastoral functions. The Services are keen to make sure that these are performed in a manner that does not interfere with military operations and in an ecumenical spirit which will lessen or exclude altogether any overt religious rivalry that might lead to dissension in the military community.

Chaplains are classed as military non-combatants and it is made clear that their protected status must not be used as a shield for military operations. According to the Geneva Conventions chaplains may not be armed and if captured may be 'retained' to meet the spiritual needs of prisoners of war of their own forces.

Gethyn Jones (1988) tells of going out and buying himself a small .25 revolver as a means of personal protection when moving from one post to another, admitting that this was a breach of the Geneva Convention "and most reprehensible." "Its use," he went on, "never became necessary, but its presence in the trouser pocket gave some measure of confidence despite its tiny calibre and consequent limited effectiveness." What follows is worth quoting in full as it appears to exemplify, in spite of the Geneva Convention, how one chaplain succumbed to the organizational pressure of the army.

> In an attempt to 'appreciate the mental strain of going on patrol in no mans land beyond the forward positions' and 'to undergo the occupation hazard, and experience the daily tensions of my companions... off came the clerical collar and battledress jacket with all its tell tale insignia and equipped with a revolver instead of a stick, the 'rookie' passed through the wire... My feelings as I took my turn to kick a door open and enter the passage or room behind, were a mixture of excitement, fear and, let it be said, guilt. The last reaction was engendered no doubt by the knowledge that I was breaking the Geneva

Convention that a chaplain should not be armed... What would have happened had a German faced me I now dread to think. That I would have pulled the trigger (had there been time) there is no doubt. I had used the revolver and rifle on the ranges and had shown some proficiency in the use of both weapons.

(Gethyn Jones, 1988, 32)

It would be naïve to imagine an exact congruence between official goals - the desired state of affairs which an organization attempts to realise, and operative goals - actual operating procedures which show what the organization does, regardless of what the official goals might say are the aims. This is further complicated by the presence in every organization - chaplaincy included - of members with an agenda over and beyond simply carrying out existing official procedures, whose behaviour can clearly be at cross purposes with stated goals of the organization. The Rev Tom Bradley, an army chaplain killed in the 1980's in a car accident, related to the author an incident vividly illustrating this phenomenon. In the early 1970's in Belfast, British Army search patrols, often at night, would enter private homes of suspected IRA members or sympathisers in Catholic areas and none-too-gently round up the occupants into one room then systematically search the property, often with considerable destruction to the contents and fabric by tearing up floorboards etc. Predictably, such activities were bitterly resented by those whose home received such a violent visitation. The Roman Catholic Chaplain to a Parachute Regiment - a man much respected but singularly gung ho, chose to accompany a search party, having removed his collar-crosses, making him indistinguishable from his fellow soldiers. During a search in which he was taking part, he was recognised and his life threatened. When in 1972 the Officers' Mess of the Parachute Regiment in Aldershot was bombed by the IRA, ironically the sole military fatality was the Rev Gerry Weston, that same chaplain who had taken it upon himself to follow his own agenda in Belfast.

A report from Richard Cleroux in Ottawa carried by *The Times*, Saturday July 6th 1996, reads

37

Newspapers led their front pages yesterday with a 1993 photograph showing a smiling army chaplain, Captain Mark Sargent, standing over a group of trussed and blindfolded Somali children holding signs that read 'I am a thief'. While there is no indication whether the captain interceded on behalf of the children, he has refused to speak publicly until he testifies later this year before a Royal Commission of Inquiry set up by the Canadian Government to investigate the Somalia affair... Under the Geneva Convention, prisoners of war - if that is what the children were - are not to be humiliated publicly.

One might imagine reading the following extract from the Unit Guide to Administration of Personnel in War, Chapter 56, that policy would have determined what chaplains actually did. Since the First World War, especially in wartime, chaplains have engaged to a greater or lesser degree in work which that paragraph would expressly forbid them and about which there has never been the unanimity of role which is outlined.

The spiritual and moral welfare of all ranks and especially the spiritual comfort of the sick and wounded are the responsibilities of the chaplains, who can make an important contribution to high morale. They will need the support and help of all commanders and staffs if their work is to achieve the maximum effectiveness. A chaplain's work is primarily spiritual and pastoral, with the basic aim of making and sustaining a soldier's religion. This leaves him no time to assume executive responsibility as welfare or entertainments officer, from which task he is expressly precluded.

The large degree of autonomy claimed by clergymen reinforced by the general ignorance in society as a whole of the role of ministers of religion, compounded by the added stress and confusion of war, led many chaplains to undertake a remarkable range of activities in the name of ministry. Beyond church and rectory in a disorientatingly organized rank-structured society, it is important for a chaplain to discover those implicit and explicit expectations necessary for survival. These the Chaplains' Department attempts to give.

The Royal Army Chaplains' Department
Chaplains' Handbook

If the Chaplains' Department sins it is by leaving nothing to Providence, nor does it believe that by grace of ordination, sincere purpose or common sense, will a man know what to do and how to behave as a chaplain, so he is issued with a 109 page 30,000 word Handbook. Of the sixteen chapters contained in the Handbook, Chapter 1 describes the organization of the RAChD as a Department within the Army; Chapter 2 speaks of chaplains' assistants; Chapters 3, 4, 9 and 10 tell of the organization of the Army itself; Chapters 5, 6, 7 and 8 show correct procedures to be followed by chaplain in personal managerial and ecclesiastical administration; Chapters 13 and 14 give methods of instruction techniques; welfare and voluntary organizations are described in Chapter 15 and the traditions of the Denominations in Chapter 16, leaving Chapter 11 which deals with Pastoralia and Chapter 12 on Religious Instruction. A total of five pages out of 110 are concerned with the specifically religious aspect of chaplaincy work.

> A chaplain holds the Queen's Commission as a chaplain [CHB 0129] A chaplain is responsible wherever he may be stationed for the spiritual welfare of all ranks and their families committed to his charge [CHB 0129 b]

Queens Regulations outlines the duties of chaplains but the Handbook states them in more detail:

> a) The conduct of Divine Worship and the Administration of the Sacraments according to the tradition of his own denomination.

39

b) The supervision of his Garrison or Unit Church with all its organizations and activities, e.g. Sunday School, Women's Guilds, Youth Fellowships etc.

c) Giving religious instruction to children in Garrison Schools.

d) The systematic visitation of families, patients in hospital and soldiers undergoing detention.

e) Carrying out the programme of Character Training for all ranks.

f) Taking an interest in the general welfare of his Unit including their social and sporting activities.

g) Accompanying troops on exercise and training in order to
   (i) master a minimum of military skills in the field
   (ii) share as fully as possible the life of the men he seeks to serve.

Remarkably little else is said regarding the duties of a chaplain, a fact which is open to a number of interpretations ranging from the presumption, by the Chaplains' Department, that any chaplain knows what to do and does it, to a quite distinctive "laissez faire" attitude, to how much or little a chaplain might concern himself with what an average layman would term religious matters. Organizationally British Army chaplaincy could be faced with enormous problems but in fact whatever problems there are in administering different religious bodies (which still preserve a degree of autonomy and final religious responsibility and authority over its various chaplains), have over time been largely overcome. It was not always so, as the following example illustrates:

> I am sorry to say that the French Church behaved very badly to us and refused after 1915 to allow us to use even ruined churches for our services... I am afraid we had the English Roman Catholic Padres to thank for the French Church's dealing so hardly with us, for it was they who stirred up the good natured French Bishops against us.
> (Horsley Smith, 1978)

40

Though there is a double control and administration, priority lies with the chaplain's religious organization outside the army, while in his everyday experience the chaplain is immediately subject to the military. Were the Church or denomination to withdraw its endorsement of a particular chaplain it would automatically result in his dismissal from the Chaplains' Department and the Army, notwithstanding how acceptable he was to the Army and the Chaplains' Department as a chaplain, confirming the primacy of the Church over the Army in recruitment and retention.

As a counterweight it should be noted that if a Church of England chaplain, or any chaplain who is married, were to divorce and remarry, though his own denomination might countenance such an act, until 1995 the Chaplains' Department would have asked him to resign his Chaplaincy commission and his Service ministry. Here was an example of an authority being exercised by the Chaplains' Department which many an individual Church no longer claimed. In spite of appearances that the Chaplains' Department in behaving this way was making a theological statement, such a reaction was at least as much influenced by presently perceived social niceties and straightforward army discipline as theological rigidity.

Some other anomalies should be mentioned. Though it might make a certain sense in those churches where there are gradations of clergy, curates, parish priests, Deans, Vicars General and Bishops, to join another organization where ranks are organizationally crucial, it is remarkable how the clergy of other churches where this is even frowned upon, so readily adopt the subject/superior roles within the Army Chaplaincy Department. Unlike his civilian colleagues, who are called by or bound to their congregations, the Baptist army chaplain is posted to and from unit churches without any consultation with those church communities, or any reference to the Baptist congregationalist policy. Some Baptists would consider the appointment of the minister to a congregation if not theologically then at least ecclesiologically decisive, yet this is apparently jettisoned with some ease by Baptist chaplains. Lest it be supposed that those churches with hierarchies or clerical superiors, Reformed or Roman Catholic, are more consistent, a minister from any of these is, during his chaplaincy, both operationally and psychologically more responsible to the army chaplaincy chain of command than he is to his ecclesiastical superiors, and what is more, the further he advances within the chaplaincy, the more it suits him that it is so, for promotion, status and salary are conferred by the army not by his church.

Though it could be stated that the Royal Army Chaplains' Department, to give it its official title, is a simple institutional response to having an army, the two succeeding chapters are intended to show with evidence of two remarkable but by no means individual viewpoints, that the role chaplains served was and is decidedly ambiguous. The evidence makes it increasingly difficult to accept the platitudinous role which runs:

> there are religious people in the army as in the rest of society;
> army chaplaincy is the institutional response to this;
> army chaplains merely serve the religious needs of soldiers.

Though the official goal, the publicly stated goal of the chaplains is 'to make and sustain christians' it will be seen that though many if not all attempted to provide religion for the religious and through enforced church attendance for the irreligious too, they provided both intentionally and unintentionally legitimacy to the enterprise, either by dislodging the priority of God by espousal of unashamed nationalism or preaching 'Jehad'. Each was an organizational endeavour to give temporal relevance to the Christian church, to be better servants of the State.

The Reverend Charles Doudney when home on sick leave from the Front preached a sermon published in the *Bath Journal*, 24th July 1915, where he says "They are not fighting alone for men, but it is a spiritual war they are fighting, side by side with God to get rid of the sin of the world." What the average soldier at the Front would have made of such an assertion is open to debate, though one is reminded of that soldier's remark who on listening to the padre's exhortation to 'fight against sin' was heard to say "You would think he would know that one bloody 'push' at a time weren't enough."

Chapter 3

The Chaplain's Role : World War I

On reporting at the orderly room of a Highland Battalion
then stationed at a home base, following a decimating
engagement at the Front, I was treated to a lecture of
twenty minutes duration from the CO upon the gravity of
the commission now entrusted to my charge and the
challenge to my manhood represented by the liabilities I
was inheriting, not from predecessors in that famous
regiment, not at all, but from the alleged mixed reputation
of Army Chaplains at large.

(Blair, 1954)

As in any organization, if an individual does not lay claim to a
precise role someone will find a role for that spare pair of hands.
The roles chaplains have undertaken have ranged from the wholly
secular to strictly religious activities and while it has rarely been the
case that a chaplain has totally abrogated his religious role, there are
numerous examples of chaplains engaging in activities which while
not inimical to their role as chaplain are only peripherally connected
with what is generally understood as a clergyman's role.

Imprecisely defined Role

22nd April 1915: I have had a somewhat strenuous and
exciting day. There is a most complete X-ray plant here,
with a specialist doctor in charge. At breakfast he
announced the assistant was ill, and as I had been through
the apparatus with him he roped me in to help. Well we
worked at it all morning and did about 12 men just in
from the last battle. Then after lunch, he had to go away
and there were six more to do. So he collared another
doctor and left us there to do the work. The other man, a
most decent chap, had helped an X-ray man about ten
years ago for a season and had forgotten all he ever knew

and said so. As to the electrical part he knew nothing. So there was I in a maze of dynamos and coils and switches and terrific high tension current. The doctor fixed the patients up and I worked the thing.

(Horne, 1995, 109)

The term resocialization describes that condition which ministers experienced on joining the Chaplains' Department in World War I when their previously accepted role and behaviour had to be redefined in the quite chaotic and frightening setting of war. In such a situation of extreme stress, the pressure of conforming to the day to day demands of the Army often led to the chaplain meeting the expectations of others rather than informing them of the parameters of his own role. The more imprecise a role the minister envisaged for himself, the more likely he was to succumb to the temptation of being useful rather than being a priest. In the situation where the priest was uncertain of his role, in which all the familiar supports of his parochial surroundings were removed, the organization determined the chaplain's role in those cases where he was not strong enough to define it himself. Monyhan (1983:119) shows one attitude

> Murray's avowed aim as a padre was service to others ('to be of use by God's help'). Church services and ministrations to the dying apart, he appears to have equated this more with the physical and material welfare of the men than with spiritual or moral guidance.

Referring to the objections voiced by those who to his mind too narrowly defined the chaplains role, Middleton Brumwell (1943:36) stated that he had always held that anything that gave a chaplain contact with the men was a benefit to his work, and while fighting shy of making him sports officer for one unit, it certainly contributed to the success of a padre if he took fair share in the organization of the social activities of the unit. Not only was he unprepared to state categorically that the organization of the social activities of the unit was not the chaplain's role, but the assertion is made that a padre's success - one wonders by what criterion - will be judged by it. Little

44

wonder that numerous chaplains failed to resist such organizational army pressure, not to say chaplaincy pressure to fulfil an army rather than a church role, and that chaplains have been given medals for doing so, reinforces that very human and understandable proclivity. The Reverend Charles Doudney, though referring also to visiting the wounded in the wards in the afternoon, describes a typical morning's work, which, by his own assertion, is intended to make clear what he has to do. The date was May 14th, 1915.

> 6.30 - called by my servant, who brings my charger round at 7 o' clock. Then a glorious ride in the great forest, whose edge is reached in five minutes. 8.30 - back and am met at the hospital by the man who takes the horse to the stable. Then comes the letter-censoring for say one or two hours until (nearly every day) an orderly appears with 'Please sir would you kindly go over to the X-ray room.' And there I work for the rest of the morning. We have photographed well over 100 cases in the past few days.
>
> (Horne, 1995, 109-110)

The reconciliation between the rival claims of the two main functions associated with being a chaplain viz. the specifically religious and the jack of all trades, Blair (1954:46) highlights:

> Out of the line in those earlier and more ill directed days, there were the compulsory church parades, the relentless call for organized sport, the running of the inevitable canteen, while in the frantic turmoil and confusion of battle, first aid to the wounded, reverent attendance upon the last rites of the fallen and hurried and heartbreaking correspondence with the bereaved at home, crowded out all other demands upon a padre's time and energies.

Again and again it appears almost taken for granted that the specifically religious activities of chaplains took second place and when objection was made, it was disarmed even by those in authority who if not indifferent to the problem refused to see it as one. One

45

senior chaplain in 1915 recorded that when his own complaint on the matter was to all intents dismissed by the Deputy Chaplain General, a Bishop Gwynne, he was cheered! In Blackburne's own words (1932:60)

> I rather moaned to the Bishop that I had to spend so much of my time looking after buns but he cheered me by saying 'Never mind, they are sanctified buns'.

The same chaplain's claim to fame was that during the Battle of Loos he took a canteen as close to the front as he could and distributed tea, bread and butter to those going forward or to the rear and claimed that in one day alone they cut up and buttered 450 loaves of bread. One may legitimately wonder what the Quartermasters department were doing, and may confidently assume that they were neither praying nor acting as locum for the chaplain. Generals then and since said the chaplains were doing a great job. When Sir Douglas Haig visited the Headquarters and the Senior Chaplain was introduced to him, he reported that Haig said, 'Tell your chaplains that a good chaplain is as valuable as a good General', an observation both flattering but ambiguous.

Paradoxical Praise of Chaplains

Field Marshal Lord Harding wrote that in all his experience in both World Wars, in the years between the wars and in the various campaigns since the end of the Second World War, the army chaplains as a whole made an invaluable contribution to the morale and comfort of the troops. He maintained it was a contribution that could not have been made by any other body of men or in any other way. "It is a good Regimental Padre, irrespective of denomination, who contributes most to the morale and comfort of the men he serves." (Smyth VC 1968:256-257). The ambiguity of what Harding precisely meant by morale and comfort, used twice, is echoed by the assertion apropos the chaplain's place at the dressing station

> At that point the chaplain can do for a badly wounded
> or dying man what no one else in that situation can do -

listen to him, write a letter for him, sometimes send
back to those at home his very last message. (Smyth
1968:165)

The assertion being that the chaplain in doing the above was doing
what 'no one else could' fails to convince. One is strongly reminded
of the words of Guy Chapman 1933 (1964 edn :6) apropos 'our bluff
Anglican' of whom he said there was a growing dislike. Chapman
claimed the chaplain had nothing to offer, but the consolation the
next man could give you, and a less fortifying one. Once again what
is specifically religious or spiritual is not mentioned. Sir Douglas
Haig was more precise in his own appraisal of what chaplains were
doing, in a private letter to the Deputy Chaplain General in France:

> August 7 1916
> My Dear Bishop,
> Very many thanks for your most friendly
> letter. I appreciate most truly your kindly appreciation
> of my efforts to help you in your great work. That the
> troops are in such splendid heart and morale and fight
> 'without counting the cost' is largely attributable to our
> chaplains who have so successfully made our men
> realise what we are fighting for and for the justice of
> our cause."

In 1934, Dean Inge noted in his Diary the opinion of Lord
Plumer, who had commanded the Second Army of the British
Expeditionary Force, that of all men, Bishop Gwynne did most to
win the war (Wilkinson 1978:127).

Allowing for the possibility of hyperbole, it is unclear what such
an assertion could mean in the mouth of a Field Marshal, especially
when in so many major histories of both World Wars the role of
chaplains is not even mentioned, unless one accepts the probability
that the Generals acknowledged that the chaplains had in fact
convinced soldiers of the equivalence of the national cause with the
will of God.

The written evidence remaining from the first World War
presents us with a puzzling anomaly. There can be no doubt that a

notable proportion of chaplains were decorated both for bravery and for devotion to duty. The numbers of chaplains killed or wounded is sufficient evidence of their closeness to the front and to the areas of danger. Precisely what they were doing there is often less clear.

> October 8th 1918: Our losses during the day were heavy. Griffiths, an outstandingly good officer, was killed, as was our Nonconformist padre. The padre should not have gone with A Company in the early morning. He was told that he would be an embarrassment to them; but he was impulsive, he insisted on going, and was killed when seeking an M.C. to please some fool of a girl in Liverpool who had taunted him with having no decoration. (Dunn, 1994, 556)

What is being referred to is less the question why ministers should be with fighting troops in wartime but what their function is when they are there. To the reader it might appear obvious why the chaplain was there, but Wilkinson (1978, 152) highlights the disconcerting complexity of his position.

> Most chaplains as Christian leaders inevitably felt more keenly than others the tremendous strain of constantly trying to reconcile their beliefs with the war. The pressure on the chaplain to become merely the mouthpiece of the military authorities was very great. Unsure of his role, treated as jack of all trades, sometimes feeling neither accepted by officers nor by men as a priest, wearied with indifference and misunderstanding, tired of innuendoes that if he was a 'real man' he would be fighting, it was tempting for him to try to solve all these tensions by a display of bellicosity.

This dilemma might have been resolved by 1996 but it certainly was not a matter of agreement in 1914. Perhaps the most famous British chaplain of World War I was Geoffrey Anketell Studdert Kennedy who asked (1919:24)

What the bloody hell is the Church doing here? An amateur stretcher bearer or an amateur undertaker? Was that all that a Christian priest could be in this ruin of a rotten civilization? I have pondered as I sat down after singing a comic song to the men at rest. An amateur comedian struggling to make men forget for one short hour the horrors in the midst of which they live and are called upon to die; always an amateur, always more or less inefficient and untrained, I was typical it seemed to me of the Church I loved and served.

Though subsequently published, the talks from which the foregoing is taken were in origin a series of lectures delivered to officers and men of the British Army in almost every part of France during the War. They give a glimpse of one chaplain's agonized search for a role in which his religious ministrations are scarcely mentioned. This same self-doubt came to the fore when he met the chaplain who was to become the most highly decorated chaplain of the 1st World War, Theodore Bayley Hardy, who in eleven months before his death at the age of 54 was awarded the Victoria Cross, the Distinguished Service Order and the Military Cross. In the record of a brief conversation between Studdert Kennedy and Bayley Hardy, the former wrote

He, (Bayley Hardy) asked me about purely spiritual works. I said there is very little; it is all muddled and mixed. Take a box of fags in your haversack and a great deal of love in your heart and go up to them, laugh with them, joke with them. You can pray with them sometimes but pray for them always. (Smyth 1968:174)

Crisis of identity, role and function, while far from singular was not universal among chaplains, though limited evidence points towards the problem being particularly acute for chaplains without a strongly sacramental ministry. To intrude a parallel illustration from a Liverpool Hospital experience in the 1960's, Roman Catholic

49

chaplains were the most acceptable and most highly regarded by Hospital staff in procedures concerning the death of patients. Death, expected or sudden, triggered hospital procedures, one of which was informing the appropriate chaplain. The Roman Catholic chaplain always went to the hospital; the other Christian chaplains sometimes went, High Church more often than Low and the Jewish chaplain on the only occasion he was sent for made it very clear that the hospital procedure on the death of Jewish patients should not affect the Rabbi. The Catholic chaplain because he always attended, gave last Rites and comforted relatives etc. was a predictable factor in the event of hospital death. The hospital organization was assisted better by the Roman Catholic organization whose own procedures concerning death dovetailed best with that of the hospital, with the consequence that the Roman Catholics appeared more organized, more professional in the eyes of the hospital authorities.

Apart from the Anglo Catholic wing, the Church of England of 1914 had made very little use of sacramental confession and extreme unction as they were then called. Chaplains were and are judged by their provision of what was expected by officers and soldiers in those situations of crisis and horror. Then as now the Roman Catholic system was far better adapted for pastoral work in crisis. As Wilkinson (1978:133) puts it

> Particularly in emergencies when little time is available sacramental rituals have an objectivity and 'professionalism' that can be more effective than improvised prayer and counsel .... In situations that are totally new and bewildering, rituals can supply boundaries and signposts so reducing the sense of chaotic novelty.

The same is said by Schneider (1989:61) that the chaplain/rabbi served as a representative of ritual and hence a physical connection between the soldier and his family. Ritual as a physical representation of religion gives a person something to connect to and identify with. Though there was no correlation between how 'religious' a soldier was and usage of ritual, it was judged to be a valuable therapeutic aid in religious terms giving soldiers a feeling of security, a coming home.

The point is made in a World War I context, by pointing out that it was understandable that Catholic chaplains at the Front were more readily accepted by the Tommy (whatever his beliefs) than their Anglican opposite number. The working class origins of Catholic chaplains meant that there were fewer of the barriers separating them from the average Tommy than beset their public school orientated Anglican counterpart. Unlike most of their opposite numbers, Catholic chaplains were respected for spending much of their time in the line, sharing the same risks and hardships as the fighting troops. There they were able to minister as priests, dispensing not fags but forgiveness: not just cheer but communion.

> Even to the non-Catholic to whom the Mass, confession and absolution were meaningless rituals, there was something commendably professional about the Catholic padre. The average Anglican by comparison seemed an amateur. (Monyhan 1983:176)

The evidence appears to show that organized religion and particularly the Church of England, again with the exception of Anglo Catholics, though so keen to fulfil its primary spiritual mission, acted in a manner characterised by amateurishness and maladroitness leading to futility in much that it tried to do, probably best exemplified in the initial prohibition of chaplains from serving close to the Front. Ironically, at the start of World War II the old controversy of where the chaplain should be arose once more. Smyth (1968) reports the curious decision that the RC chaplains who in World War I had been up at the Front when their Church of England counterparts were restricted to Rear Dressing Stations, decided in World War II that the Advanced Dressing Station was the best place.

The First World War merely served to highlight that a particular form of social ministry exercised by Church of England clergymen had been superseded. The nineteenth and early twentieth century Church had been seen as a focus of community and Anglican clergy had fulfilled many roles in an amateur and untrained capacity. They were not best served by their former association with the gentry continuing in the trenches with their identification with the officers. The age of professionalism had overtaken them and in the glare of war unprotected by traditional supports, their efforts were made to appear feeble. Not all were prepared to accept Studdert Kennedy's analysis of "very little spiritual" and "all muddled and mixed." Horsley Smith (1978:920) writing in 1930 appealed for the story to be told of the padre who was

> only ordinary and who tried to do his own work amid very difficult and discouraging conditions. Perhaps it will then be realised that a chaplain's real work did not consist in giving out cigarettes nor even in bringing in the wounded under fire (which was done magnificently and over and over again by stretcher bearers) but in ministering the Word and Sacraments and often standing in the eyes of men as a link with home and other things which were "lovely and of good report." I remember that on one occasion a padre from whom I was taking over a certain work said to me 'You will want some cigarettes to distribute. The men won't look at you unless you have them.' I felt that this was wrong and proved that it was.

In a more health conscious age, the importance of cigarettes for the average Englishman of World War I can appear overblown. Their importance in the trenches can scarcely be overemphasised. If they had not replaced sacraments, they were treated by chaplains as sacramentals. The Reverend F R Barry in 1916 said that as chaplains they did what they could to serve the troops in Christ's name and surely the distribution of cigarettes was a relevant form of the cup of cold water - and the soldiers understood why they were doing it. The typical chaplain, according to C E Montague, was a 'good sort' and was a constant source of tobacco, good at talking shop about the war, always ready to do a good turn (Wilkinson 1978:117). One is increasingly forced to the conclusion that chaplains were as closely associated with providing the consolation given by the mild narcotic as they were in providing the consolation of religion. It was not sacraments the soldiers wanted it was cigarettes. It is not as strange as it might appear but the quest for acceptance dictated to the chaplain what he should offer and it is incontrovertible that chaplains notably provided it. Whether by doing so he raised minds and hearts to God is less certain, though it is possible to think of few things less likely to inspire Godliness in soldiers, than the distribution by Fundamentalists of what were apparently book matches but on opening contained not a light but the words 'Jesus the Matchless One!'

From the documentary evidence available, religion is either taken for granted or appears only incidentally. In so many accounts by chaplains of their experiences at the Front the concentration was on secular events. One must conclude that their spiritual ministration were taken for granted. Monyhan states that religion scarcely figures in the section of Railton's autobiography covering his years as a padre, and of another chaplain the Reverend Maurice Murray, what emerges was a likeable man, modest, courageous, conscientious, but what was missing was any spiritual content. Regular services and celebrations of Holy Communion (usually to only a handful of men), ministrations to the dying, burial services, were meticulously recorded but with less comment than he attached to camp concerts and sporting events. Even in World War II the humdrum work of a chaplain is ignored and often human drama unacknowledged in autobiography. A remarkable event which must have had an abiding effect on a unit is recorded as follows

> Nobody was sorry when, in June, the unit moved to Newton Abbot. Our stay was short and marred by a tragic accident when a young trooper loosed off his tommy-gun in the billet, killing one of his room-mates and wounding two others. (Gethyn-Jones, 1988, 56)

These few lines are followed by half a page concerned with cider drinking and two pages on fishing and the sight of an otter. No attempt is made by the chaplain to interest the reader in the difficulty, even trauma, of having to minister in the aftermath of such a tragedy.

The noticable absence in chaplains' accounts of references to spiritual ministrations - purportedly the core role of a chaplain - might be construed as evidence that the chaplains themselves, in spite of assertions to the contrary, considered them incidental and certainly of interest to nobody reading a chaplain's autobiography. As there was more to be gained psychologically and socially by being a helpful friend - being of use - than by being a minister it is little wonder that many concentrated their efforts on that role. It is in this sense that officers and soldiers dictated what chaplains should do, determining their role.

The most forthright expression of what appeared as a lack of spiritual content is made by the Reverend Harold Augustine Thomas, a Broad churchman who concluded with seeming reluctance,

> I have set it on record without prejudice that the few to whom religion was anything more than a name were definitely High Churchmen and the centre of their Faith was the Sacrament of Mass, as they preferred to call it. They took a definite stand on definite teaching. The ordinary ex-Sunday school scholar and ex-choirman - the great mass of Broad or Low Church Production - were as reeds shaken by the wind or 'houses built on sand' without strength or stability. This I mention merely as a fact which came so strikingly to my notice that suppression of it would be to misrepresent deliberately, actual experience. (Monyhan 1983:110).

Though referring to soldiers rather than chaplains, the impression is strongly felt that to "the Broad or Low Church Production" little had previously been given, and in the wasteland of the trenches, their chaplains spiritually failed them. Wilkinson (1978, 234), expands on this point in greater detail:

> Evangelicals were found wanting too. The First World War found it still on the whole, clinging to most of the features of biblical literalism, unreconciled to evolution and proclaiming a stern theodicy, a type of predestination and a substitution theory of atonement. Its puritanism regarded secular life as an enemy to be

fought. Its picture of salvation and evangelism was atomistic; it had no understanding of the larger work of Christ expressed in Logos theology, and therefore could not comprehend the claims that the character of Christ was being exhibited by soldiers who were right outside any overt Christian allegiance. Anglican Evangelicals were usually among the most conservative of Churchmen politically and ecclesiastically and often held a nationalistic and Erastian view of the Church. Thinking in terms of simple antitheses between good and evil, innocent and guilty, purity and impurity, a kingdom of light and kingdom of darkness, Evangelicalism could not cope with the ethical and theological ambiguities encountered in the daily life of the soldier - the swearing, drinking, brothel-visiting soldier who might perform acts of heroism in battle, to be tender to the wounded friend and be singularly lacking in bitterness towards the enemy.

Overt Organizational Tension

Mention should be made at this point of the comparatively rare organizational tension between the Church in the Army as represented by the Chaplain General, and the Church of England as represented by the Archbishop of Canterbury. The Reverend Taylor Smith, an extreme Low Churchman and a colonial Bishop had been appointed Chaplain General in 1901. Not very well read, most of the Regular Army chaplains were of his type according to the Reverend Harold Wooley, a World War I Victoria Cross winner; many of them Protestant Irishmen. The Senior Chaplain in France was a Northern Irish Presbyterian, Dr. Simms. The appointment of Anglican chaplains was marked at first by the same partisan bias as had been shown in peacetime. Representations were made through Archbishop Davidson to Lord Halifax, that Bishop Taylor Smith had a profound aversion to Anglo Catholic "extremists" making it practically impossible for them to obtain commissions. This organizational conflict was neatly resolved by the War Office appointment of a well-liked bishop, L H Gwynne of the Sudan, as Deputy Chaplain General in charge of all Anglican Chaplains in France where most of them were serving. This meant the creation of a new office and staff entirely distinct from that of the Chaplain General's Department and meant in effect the removal of all Church of England chaplains from his command. The appointment of an alternative Senior Chaplain in France for Anglicans was unprecedented and it is to the credit of the Chaplain General that though he knew he had lost this confrontation and much against his inclination he made the system work. Dr. Simms became Principal Chaplain in France for other denominations except Roman Catholics. Blackburn, a senior chaplain, referring in his diary to a visit the Chaplain General had recently made to the front in 1916, though taken with their little chapel, reported that he did not think Taylor Smith "quite liked our Crucifix. I told him that we had learned to understand and love the Crucifix out here." (Blackburne 1932:170)

Not long into the War more sensitive chaplains realised that the hysteria and jingoism of the home front had no place on the battlefield. The Chaplain General even in his infrequent visits to France showed an attitude against which a man like Reverend David Railton could write in 1916, "It is strange how the words 'High', 'Low', 'Broad', 'Catholic' disappear out here." He recorded attending a meeting of experienced chaplains and hearing Blackburne say that the words were never used, by officers nor men: that our Englishmen do not care a pin whether a man is High or Low, Broad or Catholic, or a dissenter, whether he gives allegiance to Canterbury, Rome or to General Booth. "The biretta or the Salvation Army hat amuse equally." (Monyhan 1983:59).

It is significant that in the 191 page biography written of Bishop Taylor Smith the Chaplain General, only 9 are devoted to 1914-1918. There are two rare but revealing accounts of interviews by Bishop Taylor Smith of High Anglican Churchmen. One concerns The Reverend Railton - incidentally the originator of the idea of the Tomb of the Unknown Soldier. Railton's account appears in Monyhan (1983:83).

Bishop (a Low churchman): What would you do if a soldier came to you and said he was tired of his sins and wanted to be a Christian?

E.R: (Determined to be loyal to his Anglo Catholicity, even if it cost all): I should tell him to come and make his confession.

Bishop: Wouldn't understand what you're talking about. Go down to the Medical Officer and see if you're fit for service abroad.

The second is a highly revealing anecdote about Fr Maurice Child, an Anglican priest who was turned down by Bishop Taylor Smith when he offered his services as a chaplain. In answer to the question, What would he do for a dying soldier? he said that he would hear his confession and give him absolution. The correct answer should have been Give him a cigarette and take any last message he may have for his family. To Ronald Knox is attributed the observation that it was highly indicative of English indifferentism in matters of religion. Whether it was or not, the written evidence available repeatedly confirms the impression that chaplains at the Front in World War I were frequently sidetracked from what was their primary role. Wilkinson's 1978:126-7 reference to the above as 'a highly-coloured piece of Anglo Catholic naughtiness' is gainsaid by the weight of contrary evidence. Though they doubtless fulfilled their routine tasks of visiting men in their dugouts, burying the dead, writing to their relatives, assisting with the wounded, conducting services, there appears to have been a disproportionate amount of time spent censoring letters and fulfilling those roles which, while appreciated by the most senior officers and possibly by regimental officers in whose stead they undertook them, is evidence of the organizational experience that on the positive side, chaplains were seen to do something useful and practical which was in the Army's interest, but negatively gave themselves less time to act as ministers of Word and Sacrament which was their *raison d'être*.

Most Controversial Role

According to Zahn (1969:112)

> The military chaplain has in fact contributed to the strengthening and maintenance of the morale of the fighting forces. Even if we were to grant that this has not necessarily been the intention nor that it would be accepted by him as a definite role obligation, it remains an almost inseparable and inescapable highlight of his activities. By his very presence the pastor in uniform represents a symbol of legitimacy in the eyes of most observers, and participants, for, as the argument would go, if it were not permissible for believers to take part in the war, would the priest be there?"

It might be assumed that in the Army Chaplains' Department there is and was an organizational goal, which has been described as a desired state of affairs which the organization attempts to realise. "The sociologist of religion needs no convincing as to the importance of the military chaplaincy but for reasons the chaplain would not be too likely to consider himself." (Zahn 1971: 61.) Most major religious groups subscribe to the Christian obligation to love your neighbour and to work for peace on earth and goodwill to all under the Universal fatherhood of God. The chaplain's primary role, it might be assumed, would be to highlight those principles even in a military context. This was not how the Church of England saw its role in the First World War where this pillar of the Establishment threw itself heavily behind recruitment and the War Effort. The extent to which patriotism could distort the Christian ethos "is chillingly indicated in a sermon preached by the Bishop of London, Bishop Winnington Ingram in Westminster Abbey after a year of war. In it he called upon the nation's manhood to

> band in a great crusade - we cannot deny it - to kill Germans. To kill them, not for the sake of killing but to save the world: to kill the good as well as the bad; to kill the young men as well as the old; to kill those who have shown kindness to our wounded as well as those

fiends who crucified the Canadian Sergeant, who superintended the Armenian massacres, who sank *The Lusitania* - and to kill them lest the civilization of the world should itself be killed.... (Monyhan 1983:15-16).

When it is known that such extreme sentiments were expressed by a notable Church of England Bishop it should be less surprising to discover evidence that chaplains within the Army's organizational structure which is specifically the state vehicle of massive and organized violence, succumbed to the pressure of advocating its cause, if not instead of, then certainly as well as, carrying out their more readily recognised ecclesiastical role. The 'organization of enthusiasm', describes this concoction of patriotic duty, christianity and the rightness of the cause, advocated by the Church. Lest it be imagined that Winnington Ingram's outburst was confined to the English clergy whose profession it was to preach the gospel but who managed, without censure, to utter such blasphemies from church pulpits, Marrin (1974:111) quotes only one German Pastor Zoebel, who called for the extermination of the unregenerate

> It is this deep consciousness of our mission that permits us to congratulate ourselves and rest content with a heartfelt gratitude, when our guns beat down the children of Satan, and when our submarines - instruments to execute the Divine vengeance - send to the bottom thousands of the non-elect. We must fight the wicked with every means in our power; their suffering should give us pleasure; their cries of despair should not move German hearts. There ought to be no compromise with hell, no mercy for the servants of Satan - in other words no pity for the English, French and Russian, nor indeed for any nation that has sold itself to the Devil. They have all been condemned to death by Divine decree.

In order better to understand the attitude of chaplains especially in World War I, an attempt must be made to recapture some of the ideological mood which permeated Britain in that patriotic war which would make it more understandable that the average clergyman, in or out of the services, shared in the prevailing nationalism and was unwilling or unable to rise above it. (Wilkinson 1978) recaptures this mood superbly, but it is undeniable that there has been a concerted effort since World War I to disassociate chaplains primarily, and the Church of England as a whole, from militaristic jingoism, "An exculpatory myth is as untrue as a defamatory myth." writes Marrin (1974:179) This researcher's experience has been repeatedly to discover that any adverse criticism of the role of chaplains particularly in World War I has been met by considerable verbal hostility from other chaplains. The number of chaplain fatalities and awards is invariably and uncritically advanced as proof that they not only did what they were supposed to do but did it outstandingly. The presumption, in spite of very considerable documentary evidence to the contrary, is that their role was spiritual and religious and in doing that and only that, they lived and died.

Studdert Kennedy - Woodbine Willie

Like Marrin (1974:179) "I am well aware of the pitfalls of selecting a number of examples however large to demonstrate some social phenomenon or attitude as further investigation may uncover an equally large number to prove the contrary." Unlike Marrin, I have dared to use the example of just one chaplain as he is paradigmatic both as the most famous and best loved chaplain of World War I and as a charismatic speaker who was detailed during a considerable part of his chaplaincy in France, to preach to thousands of troops (in the Rear Areas) on their way to and from the Front. The Reverend Geoffrey Anketell Studdert Kennedy MC was a small, bat-eared, asthmatic clergyman, crudely sentimental, who even before becoming an honorary chaplain to the Forces wrote in his parish magazine for September 1914: "I cannot say too strongly that I believe every able-bodied man ought to volunteer for service anywhere. There ought to be no shirking of duty." (Purcell 1962:92). In this, Studdert Kennedy exemplified the self-imposed task of the clergy of the Church of England as a whole, who did not impose this task upon themselves for patriotic reasons alone but from the self interest viewpoint, by which they hoped by this association with the national effort, to win England back to God and to the Church. (Marrin 1974:202)

It is possible to see evidence of that 'exculpatory myth' in the wording of Purcell (1962:105)

> He (Studdert Kennedy) seems at times to have allowed himself gladly to be used as a morale booster to an extent which would certainly have been regarded as improper in a chaplain of the Second War.

Far from semblance, there is overwhelming evidence from the transcript of lectures he delivered that Studdert Kennedy resolved the conflict between the system of values proclaimed by Christianity and those engendered by the current view of patriotism, almost invariably in favour of the latter. Full analysis of the 267 page book is not possible here, but evidence is repeatedly given to illustrate the sociological expectation that individuals adjust their behaviour to suit the demands of their immediate social milieu, and that the chaplain assigned to a military unit is absorbed into the military life to the extent that his actions for the most part are approved or disapproved according to military standards of right behaviour. Reference Group theory - identification with the group with which one is most concerned - is not based on cynicism nor a pessimistic expectation of chaplains but frankly recognises the social setting in which the chaplain lives and acts to be one that is a consistently supportive force as far as the military dimension of his role is concerned which may operate to repress or otherwise place under a disadvantage the ecclesiastical dimension of the role. (Zahn, 1969:33). Amid the horror, acute stress, death and disorientation of the Front, in World War I, it is unsurprising that such identification should have taken place and would have been strange had it not been so. Evidence that it did, and to what degree, albeit in one man, now follows. That no writer in this field, with the exception of Marrin, has made much, if any, reference to the book from which the following is drawn is surprising, as it illustrates in almost every aspect and to the most extreme degree those activities and attitudes of chaplains mentioned or hinted at in other works, which were to redound to their discredit after the War.

Having baldly stated that the Church should have prevented the war and had failed, Kennedy asks what good could she do by going out into the midst of it and encouraging men to take part in it? That he maintained was what she was doing directly or indirectly, encouraging men to go on fighting and go on dying.

Remembering a lecture he heard from an army instructor on the "Spirit of the Bayonet" [Studdert Kennedy gives his address in his Author's Foreword as HQ Physical and Bayonet Training BEF] he poses himself the question how he could reconcile the Spirit of the Bayonet with the Spirit of the Cross, the Spirit of those who live to kill with the Spirit of Him who died to save. For him they are reconciled in the spirit of the Sportsman for

> the sporting spirit at its best is the highest form of the Christian's spirit attainable by men at our present stage of development and in that spirit is the only hope of civilization. The great German crime is the denial of the sporting spirit and its universal application. In international affairs, says the German, there is no sport, no rule to abide by in the game (Studdert Kennedy 1919:27-28).

Had such words in a novel been put into the mouth of a World War I chaplain they would have been criticised as anti church parody. No chaplain, it would have been claimed, ever said

> The world should be a world of sportsmen playing the game of life to rule, that is civilization and that in its final issue, is Christianity. It is the dream of the Catholic Church

Studdert Kennedy (1919:29) did and passionately meant it.

The sporting metaphor was frequently used by Studdert Kennedy. How it struck his audience, officer or soldier, can only be guessed at though Robert Graves in his Autobiography 1929 stated that Anglican chaplains were remarkably out of touch with their troops and preached on subjects and in a language quite up in the air. According to Marrin (1974:164), though it was not always recognised as a formal code, the rules for the right conduct of war were enforced for Anglican Christians by the gentleman's code of honour. He claims that it would be difficult to overstate the importance of the public school spirit, the sporting spirit and 'muscular Christianity' in forming group attitudes. The English soldier had become Tom Brown in khaki.

Few could have taken the spirit of Doctor Arnold and Rugby to such extremes as did Studdert Kennedy. More notable must be the realization that these sentiments were not the ravings of an unacceptable extremism. They struck the chords they were meant to strike and served the purpose for which they were designed.

> We believe in Sport and the sporting spirit: pure Sport is the very backbone of our British life..... Sport is the food of pugnacity, it is the natural and rational means of guarding against sensuality and sloth ... Bad sport has given us the 'slacker' and it is beyond all doubt one reason for our slowness in getting down to work on this war: he is responsible for much, and if we go on breeding him, he will be responsible for more. (Studdert Kennedy 1919:80).

Substitute the word 'Jew' for 'slacker' to hear the echo of a more sinister demagogue. Christ, complained Kennedy, was no longer recognized as 'the great white Captain', for the fighting spirit had departed from their faith. Christ was exemplar - the School Captain, the Team Captain, the Army Captain.

In the context of where and to whom such talks were given, Studdert Kennedy was an excellent apologete for the British Cause, incorporating a simplistic understanding of history with the rousing uncritical patriotism of the Irishman who is more English than the English. To the question What are we fighting for? he eulogises aggression:

> Every decent man has in him a certain amount of fighting instinct, a certain amount of pugnacity; and the British people have been called the most pugnacious people on the earth. I believe that this is true and what is more, though you may be surprised to hear it from a parson, I hope to the Lord that it will always be true, because I believe that if you destroy the fighting instinct in a man, you destroy the man and create an apology. Life will always be in some sense a glorious battle, and fortune will always favour the brave, which is just another way of saying that God has no use for the coward. (1919:36)

No shade of grey appears to have clouded Studdert Kennedy's view that one could be neutral in the war and still be a man, nor stand outside the battle and be a true lover of one's country. The choice he gave was to be a soldier or a skunk. It is difficult to understand why writers of the calibre of Wilkinson have glossed over the unmistakable espousal by Studdert Kennedy of what can only be described as an extreme view of the conjunction of Religion and Nationalism.

The significance of Studdert Kennedy's broad Irish brogue - he was born in an English vicarage and educated in England - the allusions to his frequently swearing, coupled with his small stature and nervous asthma would make his military association with "Lt Col Ronnie Campbell's team of cut throats, boxers like bombardier Billy Wells and Basham who went about giving demonstrations of physical fitness and bayonet fighting" (Smyth 1968:170) an interesting psychological study. His aim appears to have been to present himself and thereby the Church as a manly organization, fit for real men.

> To pray as Christ prayed is to pray a hero's prayer. I remember once in the line when we were being shelled very heavily, I stood beside an enormous sergeant who was a great friend of mine and on the other side of me somewhere was a chap that had lost his nerve and was whining out prayers for protection: "O God, keep me

safe!˙ O God, save me!" The sergeant was looking after his men shouting out warnings to us, and swearing steadily all the time. This fellow's prayers were getting on our nerves and at last the sergeant turned to me and said, "That chap's saying his prayers, isn't he Sir?" I said, "No he isn't sergeant, that's not prayer, it's 'wind'." (1919: 258-259).

Association with the big and tough; derision for the weak; identification with the group; getting on *our* nerves; Studdert Kennedy adopts the stance of the average soldier among soldiers - taking the line of least resistance, refusing to side with one man in his fear: not risking stepping out of line to identify with the weak even the militarily weak. Studdert Kennedy once more takes his cue from the acceptable standpoint of one organization, the Army, and uses the persuasive powers of the other, the Church, to bolster it. That Studdert Kennedy larded these talks and in all probability his sermons, with a fire-eating bombast best calculated to boost the morale of the fighting men to spur them on to the supreme sacrifice of life itself cannot be doubted, nor readily reconciled with what might have been an expected reluctance of a chaplain to advocate killing for a cause. His apparent naiveté regarding British colonial expansionism is evident when he says, that the British had acquired an enormous Empire, but history showed that that Empire had been acquired not so much by conquest as by pioneering and exploration. In contrast Prussia had made the German Empire as an Empire one of the strongest in the World.

> We told her, (Germany) that she was a fine big nation and would make a splendid second in the world; but of course this talk about being first was nonsense: we had always been there and meant to stop. (Studdert Kennedy 1919:76)

It is easy to imagine what rousing effect this chauvinism had on simple soldiers from the 'Land of Hope and Glory'.

Baum's (1975:15) comment is that bad religion promotes the structures of domination in human history. Domination rather than communion becomes the key. Man created for himself a harsh God who curses his foes and crushes their strength. He inscribes in his God the image of all his hatreds and thereby makes for himself a God who protects and promotes his wars, his dominations, his conquests. The strongest and subsequently most damaging criticism made of church and chaplains was the reprehensible association and admixture of religious language with militaristic objectives which lent a spurious legitimacy to the military endeavour and a curiously militaristic bias to religious language not intentionally literally bellicose. "Fight the good fight with all thy might" has significantly different overtones when, on the one hand, sung by a gathering of a Sewing Guild and on the other by a group of soldiers before going into battle.

> Ever and always I can see set up above this world of ours a huge and towering Cross with great arms held out east and west from the rising to the setting sun, and on that cross my God still hangs and calls on all true men to come out and share His sorrow and help save the world. In August 1914 God called in a voice like thunder. He called to England across the narrow stretch of sea, 'Come out! come out! Come out from home and comfort. Come out to right the wrong. Come out and share my sorrow and help to save the world.' God called and England answered. Thank God England answered and simply said, 'I come.'" (Studdert Kennedy 1919:130-131).

He goes on to suggest that each new cross erected above the grave of a soldier was a sign that another soul had joined the army of Redemption and had suffered with his master to uplift and heal the world. More extremely still he claimed they 'died with God to save the world - they live to work with him.' Baum (1975,75) would deny this the name of religion. It is the deformation of the truth for the sake of social interest; it is ideology, the defence of power and privilege distorting the image of reality, which distortions take place through mental processes that remain largely unconscious. "According to the biblical account the social sources of the corrupting religious trends are the protection of the community against hostile forces and the defence of its power elites. The corrupting trends tend to attach people uncritically to their tradition, prevent them from coming to self knowledge, defend the authority of the dominant classes, create a false sense of superiority over others and produce dreams of victory over outsiders."

One notable passage encapsulates the entanglement of religion, patriotism, militarism and authoritarianism,

> You don't fail in your duty to the Army because your captain is a fool; if you did in time of war, you would be shot, and you'd deserve it too. The British Army is what soldiers make it and so is the Christian army too. It is always time of war with the Church and you have no right to stand outside and criticise: you must come inside and fight. The Church of Christ is not a perfect army, she has her glaring faults, her officers are not all perfect Christians some of them are perfect fools; but I believe in the Church of Christ, I believe that she will conquer, and because I believe I fight, and I believe in fighting for Christ and His Church, I am fighting for old England and the Freedom of the world. (Studdert Kennedy, 1919:91-92)

England becomes not just ones country but the embodiment of freedom and democracy so the duty to defend England is identified with a duty to defend freedom, both of which are presented as if mandated by God Himself. Christ's support for His Church against its enemies is made to imply a similar relationship between Christ and freedom-defending England. Theology, if it can be called such, is harnessed to the National Cause and mightily distorted. Did it flash through any mind that the Kaiser might have been a second Cyrus come to humble the too proud British Empire?

Those chaplains who failed to see a clear religious role for themselves were given a role, especially in World War I. According to Purcell, the charge chiefly preferred against the chaplain seemed to have been one of inadequacy. Some of the criticisms were more touching than were perhaps intended. Siegfried Sassoon in *Memoirs of an Infantry Officer* in a few clear lines painted a picture which haunts the mind. The scene was the casualty clearing station; with many wounded covered in the blood and filth of their condition. One person on that horrific stage who seemed to have no part to play was a chaplain, discovering the inadequacies of the ministry of the Church of England. Had he a role, asked Sassoon. One Wonders. Across the years, something of the plight of that unhappy man comes through the print. (Purcell 1962:101)

Studdert Kennedy has been held up as an exceptional chaplain. The evidence from his own writing - transcripts of lectures he gave - points to his having adopted a role which primarily emphasised the Army's aims and objectives. There is no question of denying the heroism and sacrifice of any chaplain, least of all Studdert Kennedy, who was awarded the Military Cross at Messines in 1917. But he himself gives incontrovertible evidence of what has often only been stated as a suspicion; that chaplains adopted the role of morale-sustaining propagandists for the national cause. When it is known that most of the higher commanders were emphatic that a good chaplain was of the greatest value in raising the morale of the troops, whereas a bad one was worse than useless, it is significant in the light of the morale-sustaining work of Studdert Kennedy that no attempt was made to enlarge on the criterion they used to judge what made a good or a bad one: it was obvious. "Tommy does not want religion. I don't persuade him" wrote one chaplain. (Wilkinson 1978:143). Many therefore set about doing something else that was appreciated.

Though it has been possible to survey the role of many British Army Chaplains in World War II this study has been confined to discover whether any of those extreme attitudes evidenced from the previous chapter on World War I were apparent or operational in World War II. Once more the evidence is provided mainly by one man who though not as charismatic a figure as Studdert Kennedy was more influential in the Chaplains' Department as he subsequently became Chaplain General, Frederick Llewelyn Hughes.

CHAPLAINS AT THE FRONT:
AN ASSEMBLY OF DENOMINATIONS

Rev. E.L. Watson,
Senior Baptist Chaplain

Rev. J.M. Simms DD KHC,
Presbyterian
Principal Chaplain

Bishop Taylor Smith, Chaplain-General

Rev. O.S. Watkins,
Senior Wesleyan Chaplain

Rev. E.G.F. Macpherson
Senior Church of England Chaplain

WOODBINE WILLIE

The Reverend Geoffrey Studdert Kennedy, MC.
1883 - 1929

Left: G.A. Studdert Kennedy in uniform. *Below*
G.A. Studdert Kennedy after the war. It is not
known when it became usual for former chaplains
to wear ribbons of their decorations and campaign
medals on their preaching scarves.

He would, 'stand on a box and announce to the crowds of soldiery that he was
about to sing *Mother Machree* for the sons, *Little Grey Home in the West* for the
husbands, *The Sunshine of your Smile* for the lovers. Afterwards he would offer
to write home for them, and was seen to be doing so, surrounded by a throng
pressing in on him. And when the time came for them to go, he would be by the
train as it pulled out until he was left, heavy with his thoughts, to watch its
vanishing tail-light.'

From *Woodbine Willie* by William Purcell, Mowbray 19

BISHOP LLEWELLYN H. GWYNNE

Inset left: Presentation portrait by Francis E. Hodge. *Below*: The Bishop as Deputy Chaplain-General in France.

A BOMBING SCHOOL FOR CHAPLAINS

what?" exclaimed [General]Plumer.

ynne went on to elaborate his idea and said how necessary it was to bring back chaplains from time to time for a "gingering up". "You have refresher courses machine gunners and others. Why should I not have one for chaplains?" mer thought the idea was a good one and offered to put at his disposal a teau with extensive grounds and beds for twenty chaplains.

From *Pastor on the Nile* by H.C. Jackson, S.P.C.K., 1960

The Reverend Theodore Bayley Hardy
VC DSO MC
1863 - 1918

Facing page, above: H.M. King George V presents the Victoria Cross
Theodore Bayley Hardy at Frohen-le-Grand, the 3rd Army Commander's HQ, c
9th August 1918.. Compare this with the painting by Terence Cuneo, above,
which there is a significant degree of artistic licence. Elizabeth Hard
photographed in front of the painting and also visible in the background of th
photograph, was not best pleased that Cuneo had seen fit to depict Hardy wit
mud on his boots, as she had spent much of the previous evening polishing ther
Cuneo's brief was, however, in common with that of all war artists, to convey
sense of the action in which Hardy had been involved, hence the equall
inaccurate depiction of Hardy wearing a helmet. A real sense of the action
conveyed by the photograph below on the facing page; Hardy can be seen right c
centre, peering over the shoulder of a German prisoner and a British Corporal at
wounded man on a stretcher.

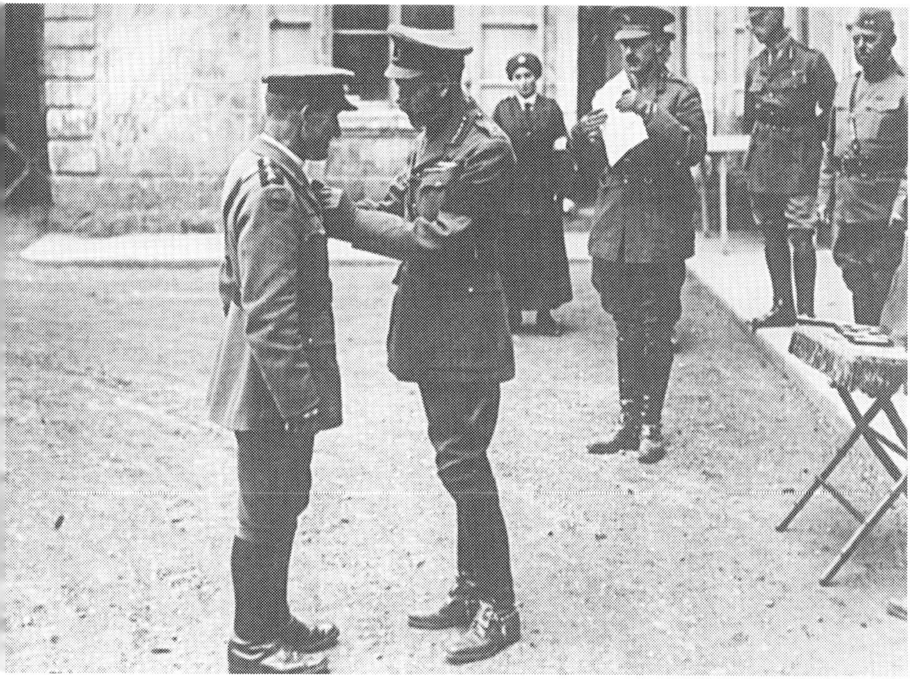

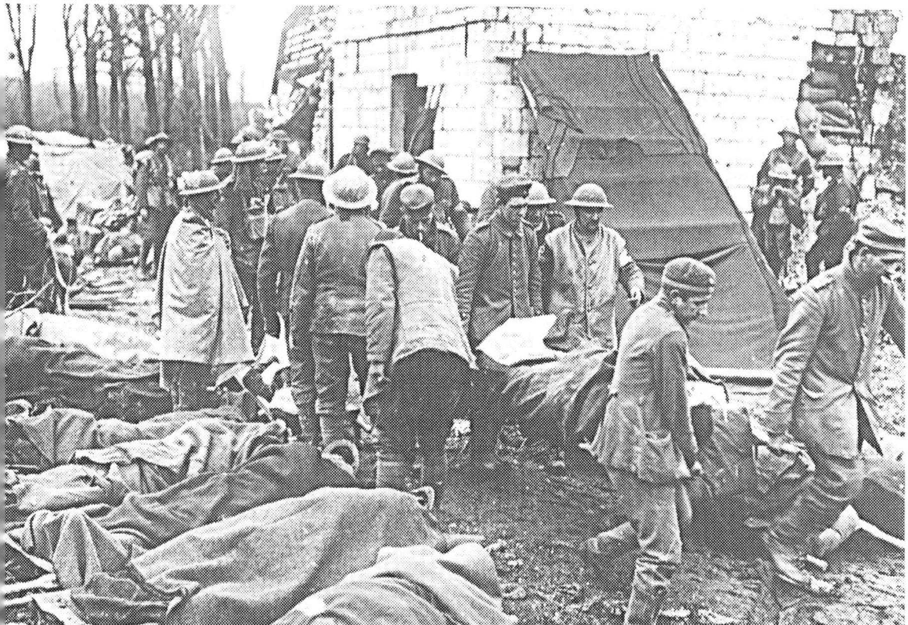

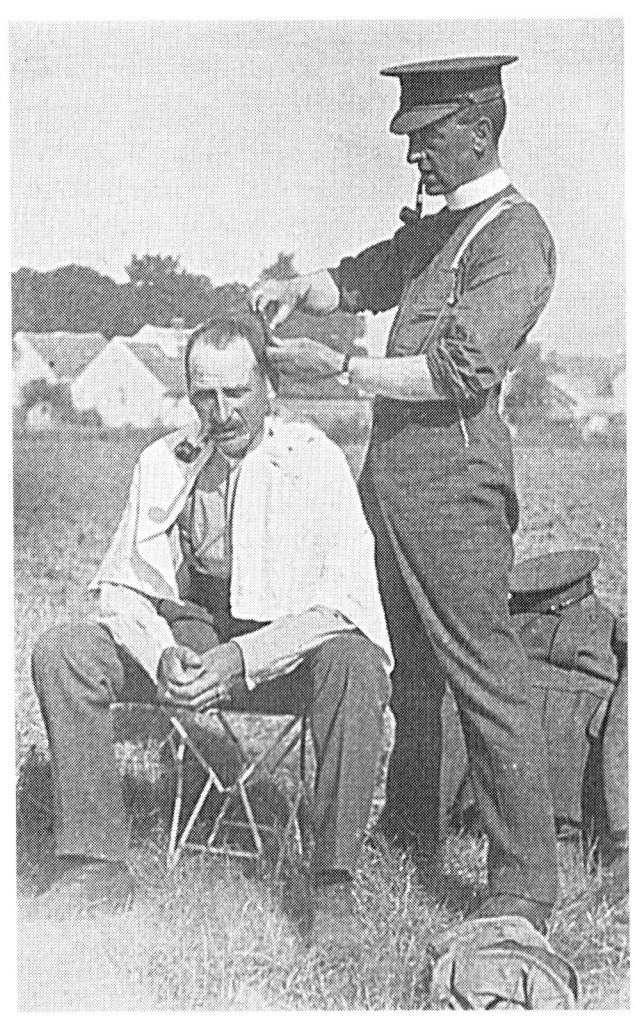

'ONE MAN IN HIS TIME FILLS MANY ROLES'

"...today I filled the role of a barber. My subject was the Rev. O.S. Watkins, who placed himself in my hands with great confidence, although the photograph suggests misgivings on his part. My work was voted so satisfactory that I was there and then appointed honorary barber to the officers' mess."

From *The Church in the Fighting Line*
by Douglas P. Winnifrith, Chaplain to the Forces,
Hodder and Stoughton, 1915

The Reverend Owen Spencer Watkins
Wesleyan Chaplain to the Forces

Owen Spencer Watkins (encircled above) is shown with a group of officers of 4th Field Ambulance. The Rev. D. P. Winnifrith is seated second from the right in the middle row (see facing page). Watkins found himself responsible for the day-to-day morale of men of all denominations, organising football matches as well as ministering to the wounded and dying.

> Christmas 1914: "In the trenches there was an informal truce; few, if any, shots were fired, both British and German made merry, and celebrated the coming of Him who was the Prince of Peace by abstaining from all hostile acts. But far away, like distant thunder, came the angry growling of heavy guns in action, and we knew that in other parts of our far-flung line there was no peace. (*With French in France and Flanders*, Owen Spencer Watkins, Charles H. Kelly, !915.)

'EVERYBODY'S BISHOP'

Left and below: Bishop J. Taylor Smith, KCI CVO DD, not a popular man, progressed from humble beginnings to become successivel Bishop of Sierra Leone and in 1901, with the support of Queen Victoria, Chaplain-General o the Army. According to Major General E.O Hay, [*J. Taylor Smith, Everybody's Bishop* Maurice Whitlow, Lutterworth Press, 1938] 'i was put to him that, being a great missionary he might be nominated to a position whicl would give him the best chance of dealing witl the largest missionary society in the world namely, the soldiers of the British Army.'

The notion of the British soldier as missionary was an enduring one but curiously unimpeded by most of the evidence which pointed quite in the other direction. The soldier's link with Church and chaplain was discovered to be alarmingly tenuous in World War I and subsequently, yet the missionary myth continued to be peddled.

BURIAL IN THE TRENCHES

An army chaplain conducting a burial service in a trench near Guillemont, September 1916. The shamrock shoulder patch would suggest that he belonged to an Irish regiment, hence the traditional assumption that he was a Catholic priest.

Soldiers conducting a service on board a troopship. They are most likely Methodists bound for service in the South African War, 1899-1902. This makeshift gathering offers an interesting contrast to the traditional concept of the Drumhead Service, with obligatory chaplain and regimented attendance.

The Reverend Arthur Male

Arthur Male served with great distinction during the whole of the Afghan War, 1878-9 and in India. Note that although he is a chaplain he carries a holstered revolver, showing that the disassociation between combat officer and chaplain, subsequently spelt out in Geneva Conventions, was not then in operation. Male was Gazetted to minister to Wesleyan troops, not by the War Office but only by the Calcutta Government. He was a victim of what O. S. Watkins called 'the anomalous position at that period held by the Wesleyan Church'. It was recommended, in respect of ministry, by the Army and Navy Sub-Committe that ministers such as Male were to be accorded 'transport, ration &c. but not pay'.

THE REVEREND E. J. KENNEDY
Chaplain Major to The Expeditionary Force

"This is the happy warrior, this is he
Whom every man in arms should wish to be."

These lines were quoted by the editor of Kennedy's book *With The Immortal Seventh Division*, Hodder and Stoughton, 1916. In the preface to this book the Bishop of Winchester refers to Kennedy's 'commanding stature, and fine physical manhood', and an ordinary soldier wrote, after Kennedy's death, that he was 'a real manly Christian gentleman'. This photograph represents the accepted ideal of an Army Chaplain in those days, a man on equally good terms with Church, State and the ranks.

Two contrasting images of the chaplain's role at the Front. Above: A drawing by A. Michael of a Padre holding a Sunday Evening Service in the field. Below: The Bishop of London (magnified) at the Front at Easter, addressing men of the Army Service Corps from a transport cart.

'Back in France [Siegfried Sassoon] attended a Church parade addressed by a Bishop in uniform (a fact which speaks for itself) who told them they were like the early Christians being thrown to the lions and that Christ was not 'the effete figure in stained glass windows but the Warrior Son of God'. (Wilkinson, A. *The Church of England and the First World War*, London SPCK, 1978)

FIELD AMBULANCE

Dranoutre Church Hospital

Two interestingly dissimilar depictions of the church hospital at Dranoutre, a small Belgian village where a Field Ambulance was established. O.S. Watkins wrote: "We daily experienced one of those strange contrasts of war which to us have become commonplaces - at one end of the church the wounded and sick lying in the straw, at the other the officiating priest at the High Altar, surrounded by the worshipping villagers."

**The Last Absolution of the Munsters at Rue du Bois, 1915
by Fortunino Matania**

This picture represents an actual incident in France in May 1915 when the second battalion of the Munsters suffered very heavily at Rue du Bois, in the Pa de Calais near Arras. The battalion had been reinforced at that time by late recruits after it had been cut to pieces during the retreat from Mons. There the Munsters were left as rearguards to one of the British Army Corps and they succeeded in holding up the advance of greatly superior German forces. But the action in Rue du Bois in May was only one of many local attacks which ended disastrously through lack of sufficient support.

Colonel Victor Rickard, who was then recently appointed to Command, was killed in the attack, as was his Adjutant, Captain Filgate. They are both represented here beside the Chaplain, Father Francis Gleeson, who is shown giving the Last Absolution to the Regiment as they halted in twilight by a wayside shrine on the 8th May on the way up to the attack at Aubers Ridge on Sunday 9th May 1915. After the Absolution the whole Regiment, with head bared, sang the *Te Deum*, the great Thanksgiving. In the short period of the attack the Munsters lost nineteen officers and 374 men, eight of whom were taken prisoner.

Amongst the many war pictures of those years this dignified painting by Matania was perhaps the most widely reproduced. Matania was at that time the chief artist of the weekly *Sphere* which was edited by Clement Shorter. He got Matania to paint this picture as a Christmas Supplement to the *Sphere* and it was also used as a Supplement to the *Weekly Freeman*. Matania exhibited ten times at the Royal Academy between 1908 and 1922.

REFERENT POWER AMONG
'THE GRAND BROTHERHOOD OF CHAPLAINS'

Left: The Very Reverend Frederick Llewelyn Hughes, CB CBE MC TD MA, when he was Chaplain General. *Above:* Field Marshal Montgomery with Rev. Frazer McLuskey, 'the parachute padre' (behind) and Rev. Canon J. Knox. It was Hughes who coined the 'Grand Brotherhood' phrase, although his relationship with Monty set him distinctly apart from his brethren.

every opportunity Hughes included in what he wrote a reference to his own ationship with the Commander by referring to himself as 'General ontgomery's Chief Padre' or by claiming his support. What is significant is that ighes did this in a way that no other senior officer either needed or chose to do. ey enjoyed an organizational authority given them by their rank and pointment. The prestige and power Hughes gained was greatly enhanced by the teration of his association with Monty and is an excellent example of a form of ferent Power, which can be defined as the influence B has over C because of s identification with the very powerful A.

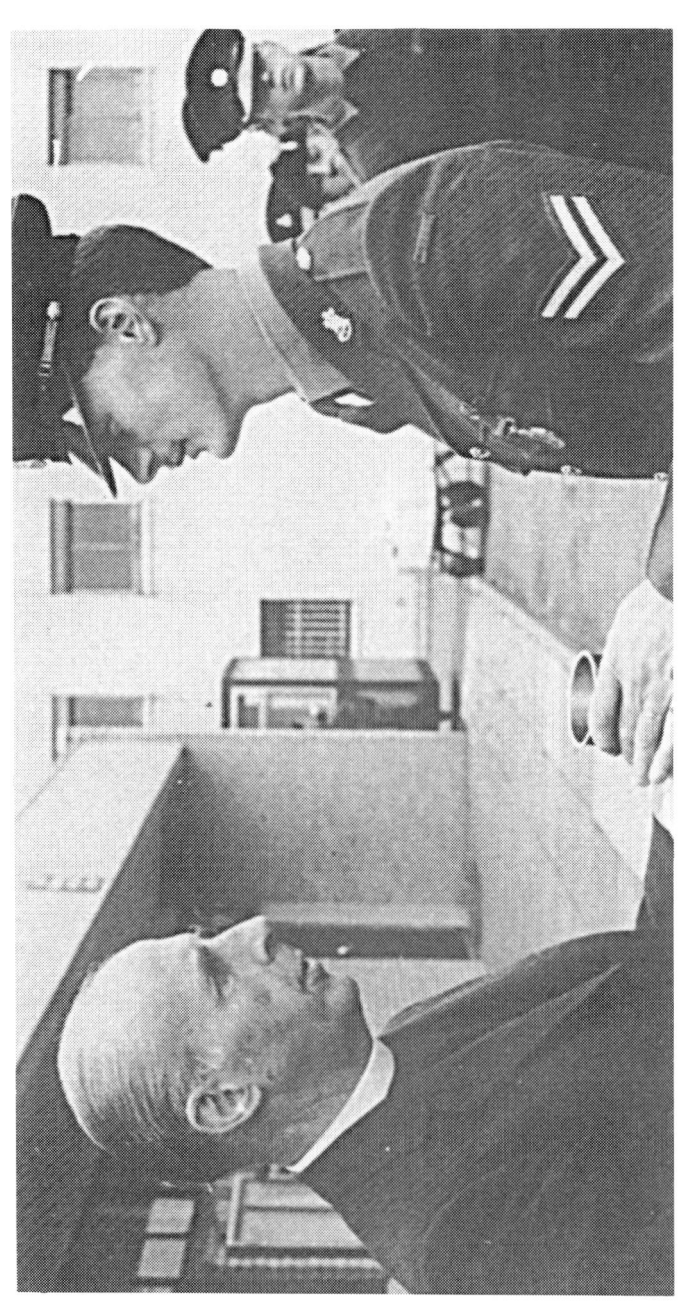

**The Venerable Archdeacon W.F. Johnston, CB QHC MA
Chaplain General 1980 - 1987**

The Chaplain General presents a prize to Corporal 'Snowy' Braddon.

The Reverend James Harkness, OBE QHC MA
Chaplain General 1987 - 1995

On the retirement of The Venerable Archdeacon Frank Johnston (facing page) in 1986, past precedent was overturned by the appointment by the Army Board of The Reverend James Harkness, a Minister of the Church of Scotland, significantly also an Established Church. Few if any questioned James Harkness's competence - he was after all the Deputy Chaplain General - but considerable misgivings were expressed over the appointment, by the Church of England establishment both inside and outside the army, who criticised what they saw as an encroachment upon a tried and tested, equitable historical practice.

It was reported that the Bishop of the Forces addressed a meeting of Church of England chaplains and stated that the appointment of the Reverend Harkness should be opposed at every turn, for, unless some protests were registered 'they would be offering the appointment to Roman Catholics next!' Though the appointment of a non Anglican Chaplain General was unimaginable to many British Anglican chaplains, the appointment as Chaplain General, of chaplains of various denominations, has proved workable as instanced by the United States Army from 1920 until 1980 where there has been 13 Chiefs of Chaplains, 4 Baptists, 1 Southern Baptist, 3 Roman Catholic, 1 Congregationalist, 1 Episcopalian, 1 Lutheran and 2 Methodists. Of course the United States does not have a state religion.

As the office of Chaplain General is administrative and impinges only peripherally on the day to day lives of chaplains, the change in leadership has made no significant difference to how the Chaplains' Department is run. (Incidentally, Dr. Victor Dobbin, an Irish Presbyterian, succeeded James Harkness as Chaplain General in 1995.)

The Reverend Dr Victor Dobbin
MBE QHC DD
Chaplain General 1995

He joined the RAChD in 1972 and has served in Germany
and the UK including Ireland. Dr Dobbin has been
instrumental in fostering ever closer links between the
Unified Branch of the RAChD and the Roman Catholic
chaplains.

Chapter 4

Between the Wars and World War II

Search for a Role

Towards the end of the war they entered a French cheese
shop. Brie was suggested. The shopkeeper was not sure
they wanted a whole Brie. The chaplain stepped forward
to explain that it was for the Mess.
"C'est pour la Messe"
Wide eyed, the shopkeeper replied
"Monsieur, Quel Religion".

Of (Travis) I have never seen much of a spiritual life in
him. He has been the Canal Grocer and has not really
recovered from it.

(Hughes,1943)

The abiding influence of the Anglican clergy and their success in
recruiting fighting men was remarkable in the light of the fact that
organized religion had been declining for at least half a century. In
their preaching they used emotive words which combined with
language calculated to appeal simultaneously to emotion, religion
and patriotism were described as masterpieces of the salesman's art.
Whatever the criticism aimed at the Church of England as a whole,
as a consequence of their World War I activity, the recruiting spirit
of the Chaplains' Department was undiminished.

A singular article from the Chaplains' Department Journal
complained that "the Churches are not doing all they might do to
encourage recruiting" and regretted that not all clergymen had been
helpful when what were known as Recruiting Services were held in
various towns. At least one chaplain had adopted the role of
Recruiting Sergeant, though how representative the view expressed
was that of the Department as a whole can only be guessed. The
presentation of Tommy Atkins as torchbearer for Christianity would

remind one that the Church and the Army report of 1919 and the accusation of being out of touch had not been heeded

> It is simply amazing the ease with which the British private soldier makes himself understood, liked and respected by the foreigner. He does not talk religion to the native, that is the necessary work of the missionary, but by his ordinary daily life, by the practice of simple Christian virtues which are so much part of his being - he is scarcely aware that they are virtues - he sets an example to the natives to which they readily respond. (Bull, 1926:185)

This alarmingly idealized view of the British private soldier is accentuated when compared with the stark realism acknowledged even by Studdert Kennedy who stated that the prevalence of venereal disease, both gonorrhoea and syphilis, among the troops was a continual source of anxiety and distress to those who led the army and the numbers 'knocked out' were sufficient to have made a difference in military operations. (Studdert Kennedy 1919:102). During the war, chaplains had been forced to confront the reality of rampant venereal disease, prostitution and the use of 'disorderly houses'. With the return of peace, the myth was peddled that Tommy had an instinctive desire to be clean in body and soul and was, unbeknown to himself, a religious missionary.

The author of the editorial note in The Chaplains' Department Journal July 1926 saw a particular role for chaplains in the General Strike, which was nothing more than the use of Army chaplaincy as a tool in the furtherance of social control. Every year saw a very large number of men entering the Army, and annually there was a corresponding return to the ordinary life of citizens. Through the Parade Service and other opportunities of military life, they could be reached by the ministrations of the chaplains and very much could be achieved by word and action to abate bitterness and to promote reconciliation and kindly feeling between various classes in the community. The yearly return of thousands of men resolved to exercise a kindly and Christian influence upon the relations of the different elements which constituted the nation 'would be a priceless benefit to the State'. By the furtherance of that aim, the chaplains were in a position to render 'an inestimable public service.' 'The fostering in civil life of those friendly and genial relations binding all ranks of the Army, which were so potent a factor in the success of our arms in the European War, were what was needed', concluded the editorial. Significantly the call is not for social justice in an order fit for heroes, but to render 'inestimable service' - 'a priceless benefit to the State'. It is not surprising that a call for greater equality did not come from chaplains, privileged members of the most rigidly rank structured organization within a still strongly hierarchical society.

World War II Role : similar pressure, similar reaction

The overall organizational state of the Chaplains' Department at the beginning of World War II was a considerable improvement on that of 1914. (Gwynne 1923:186)

> had no doubts that by 1915 those who were really responsible for completing the organization were the Generals in the field. It was they who maintained that if the chaplains were to pull their weight and be a spiritual force as well as a valuable factor in keeping up the morale of the fighting men, they must fit in as a piece of the great war machine and be as effectively organised as any other part.

Here is an example of an accepted distinction between the role of "spiritual force" as well as "valuable morale booster." Though there are instances where it might have been argued that it was specifically and only by their spiritual ministrations that chaplains became morale boosters, here is acknowledgment of their role as both spiritual force and morale booster. Venzke (1977:37) quotes a chaplain in 1945

> Chaplains are not in the Army because government is primarily interested in the saving of men's souls. The chaplain shares the mission of all other arms of the

71

service to strengthen the will to victory..... Religion can and does make souls strong for battle.

It seems to be its utilitarian purpose which has favoured religion in the Army since Wellington wrote in 1811

> not only from the desire which every man must have, that so many persons as there are in the Army should have the advantage of religious instruction, but from the knowledge that it is the greatest support and aid to discipline and order. 1968:38)

The evidence becomes clear that it was the organizational objectives of the Army that was meant when it is known that Earl Haig, the Commander in Chief, and his subordinate commanders considered chaplains "of the right sort" were quite invaluable in inspiring the fighting men but, if they were not of the right sort, they were worse than useless.

The wartime role of the chaplain had never been precisely defined with the consequence that any task undertaken could subsequently be asserted to him to be part of his role. The obvious role of ministry of Word and Sacrament included a provision of religious ritual in worship, sacramental acts, ministry to the wounded and bereaved by letter writing and above all, being with the army, subsequently defined as ministry of presence. Numerous secular activities were imposed or adopted freely, ranging from instructor in anything from sharpshooting to Swedish PT, educator, stretcher-bearer, medical assistant, provider of extras, cigarettes, food, recreation and refereeing, organiser, censor of letters and morale builder, to gravedigger and mess secretary. Those reluctant to adopt those secondary roles so much commented upon after World War I were not helped by semi-official Chaplaincy publications suggesting a sort of *noblesse oblige*.

The Reverend Kenneth Oliver (1968:18) found at the start of World War II that among many army chaplains there was a reluctance to get involved in activities that were not specifically religious. He felt that he should be concerned with every aspect of the soldiers' lives and put at their disposal whatever abilities he had.

He found, unsurprisingly to the historical onlooker, that a good deal of his time was taken up running entertainments and taking part in games and sports. In that way he claimed he made friends with soldiers who would never have considered calling on his services as a clergyman.

Making friends, though a promising start, appeared as an end in itself for Oliver who was astute enough to recognize that one of the temptations of a chaplain was to make friends with the officers at the expense of getting to know the other ranks. His book gives strong support to the suspicion that chaplains, having heard of the activities of World War I chaplains, concentrated on the establishment of friendship as an initial link. That this opening gambit more often than not led the chaplain up a *cul-de-sac* of being satisfied that he was thought of as 'a good egg' seem to have been lost on them. They were being useful, busy and they were, they believed, liked.

It was not as if he was unaware of criticism aimed at such endeavour:

> The regimental canteen became a feature of the chaplain's duties and although some poured scorn on the Holy Grocer, I knew I was making a valuable contribution to the welfare of the troops and their morale while relieving an officer for more warlike duties. (Oliver 1986:77)

As in the splendid efforts of World War I chaplains to replicate the Quartermaster's role, here again is a clearly stated objective which seems happily oblivious of the truth that none of those officers, whose less warlike roles the chaplain had undertaken, reciprocated by taking the odd service or preparing the difficult sermon. The obvious question of who was undertaking the spiritual ministrations in the absence of the chaplain simply does not occur. As if to illustrate that virtue was its own reward, Oliver was 'fortunate enough' to be invited to live in 'A' Mess with the Divisional Commander largely because he could make up a Bridge foursome with the General, who doubtless considered him an excellent fellow and a fine chaplain but, it might be contended, for reasons quite other than his notable fulfilment of any specifically religious role.

Far from there being a disinclination to get involved in any activities that were not specifically "religious", chaplains such as he, favoured such activities above any other. As is clear, Oliver found plenty to occupy his time, none of it religious, becoming sports officer, entertainments officer, trouble shooter, mess secretary, provider of a regimental canteen and a host of other activities, including bridge partner to the Divisional General - all of which would doubtless have ensured that at least by the Army he was extremely well thought of but his extraneous activities reduced any time he might have given to his more specific religious ministry. Oliver perfectly exemplified the chaplain described by Sinclair (1941:13)

> We may be hail-fellow-well-met - 'good mixers' as they are called - loving human life in all its varied many-sidedness .... man among men. We may be all that and yet complete failures as chaplains. We may be able to run a whist drive, organize a concert, run a magnificent canteen, always have a cheery word for everybody, be able to play bridge in the mess with the Colonel and yet be complete "washouts" as regards our job, because we are not bridges, we are piers. We are attached to the human but we never cross the gulf to the divine.

Frederick Llewelyn Hughes

The defects in the policy of being all things to all men were seen by some and warned against. It was an easy and cheap road to popularity. It took a man of the calibre of Hughes, subsequently Chaplain General, to state to his chaplains with 8th Army in North Africa that they had a unique role about which the Army, not to say chaplains themselves, had been unclear. With Montgomery's backing Hughes made the Army understand what were the chaplain's requirements and what his objects were. He insisted that the

74

chaplains themselves should understand their work both spiritually and practically.

Hughes, on his appointment by Montgomery, wrote a letter to "All Chaplains (other than RC) Eighth Army" setting out how he saw that the task of leading their common effort to bring the strength and goodness of the Christian faith to all ranks of the Eighth Army had fallen suddenly on him .... and then proceeded to present the war as a crusade writing that the Army Commander and those near him knew the worth to that Army of a deep and general sense that they were gathered to battle in the service of God. He continued

> We do not hold the faith for military reasons, but because the Word is true, the Sacraments of real effect, and all adrift from their best selves apart from God. But we bring it to this Army with a special gladness because men will do their stern and present duty better with its just Purpose set before them and the light of their high calling shining in and on them. (Hughes 1942)

The link between Nationalism and religion is once more made. "A soldier who fights for the British Way of Life serves God and us, for he protects the freedom of the Church." Hughes (1942) provides reminders of that fanciful out-of-touch language of World War I chaplains.

> These things are primary -- to fill this dusty desert with soldiers of the City Beautiful, who know and serve its King, and make a broad track of friendship for the traffic of ideas and ideals.

There is ample evidence from the writings of Hughes, who had been a combatant subaltern in World War I, that the ways of thinking about that war were carried over into attitudes about World War II. It is not known whether he ever heard Studdert Kennedy but there are quite close resonances between some of Hughes' language and that used by Studdert Kennedy. Only 25 years separated 1917 from

1942 with only a slightly toned-down version of what was given in 1917 being written and heard in 1942.

The assertion is remade that the "clear purpose (of the chaplains) is to assist the inspiration of the Army." (Hughes 1944a) What was considered suitable two years before in North Africa reappears in this publication with, if anything, less reticence than before, about the equation between our war and God's war. Authority once again was used in support of Hughes message. The Army Commander (Montgomery) and those near him knew the widespread worth to an army of a deep and widespread faith that they were gathered to battle by God Himself, wrote Hughes. They knew also that the faith was not held for military reasons.... but the Faith transforms the character of military effort, brings men to war for righteousness sake, sets a just purpose before them, and the light of a high calling in them. The influence of Oliver Cromwell is present though not acknowledged as he continues

> Let no pride or folly or slackness hinder our going humbly to God, seeking to consecrate ourselves, asking Him to accept our service and to grant us the aids and energies required for victory. Then we may hope to take the field as instruments of Almighty God's dominion with our morale planted securely on the rock of His calling and His might. (Hughes 1944)

Unambiguously utilitarian he states "The padre's way to an army's heart is through conviction that religion assists its fighting." Lest it be believed that the spirit of Henry Newbolt had been laid to rest at the Somme, and no-one any longer attempted to 'Play up! Play up! and play the game!' (Palgrave 1906) Hughes (1944) says

> God's ways are perfect and described in the Bible. Get every man to accept them as the rules of his game and all the conflict of a rough jostling family will be resolved by reference to an accepted standard.... and everyone's conscience is a godly referee.

Montgomery himself might have written the final line, unmistakable in its punchy vagueness, "We foster the family ideal in its purest form. It will then have a terrific morale, based on respect for first class standards." (Hughes 1944).

Other chaplains like Hughes saw a useful, and from the Army's point of view, very acceptable role for the Chaplain as morale booster, and whether the distinction between 'moral' and 'morale' was unclear to the writer himself, Middleton Brumwell (1943:52) chose to commingle them in what he wrote. Having stated that war was being waged on a moral issue, he continued by saying that those who strove to overcome (the immorality of Nazism) must maintain the highest moral standard and immediately concluded that "The development of morale is a vital object of training", treating 'moral' and 'morale' as synonyms, seemingly oblivious to the fact that the high morale of those in a pirate ship about to rape, pillage and loot has no connection with the highest moral standards.

Hughes ability to see the hand of God with the British Army in battle was undiminished by time. On the Anniversary of the first day of the Battle of Alamein, Hughes, as Assistant Chaplain General, wrote,

> It was a formidable task, but we had confidence. We had the Cause, the Leadership, the Men, the Stuff and we had more: we had the consciousness that God was calling us. The Army Commanders zero-hour Prayer clinched it. 'May God, Mighty in Battle, grant us the Victory!' Seldom can an Army have gone into battle more genuinely consecrated." (Hughes 1943)

Disregarding the unblushing sycophancy, did Hughes really believe that the pre-battle prayer of Montgomery, not his three-to-one superiority in Armour, was decisive? This is dysfunctional ministry when assertions are made which are patently fanciful yet purport to describe a religious reality. It might be true that "The historical factuality about any story is not the most important thing about it" (Young and Wilson 1986:29) but it can be 'quite up in the air' to see God as a sort of reserve Battalion ever in support of British arms.

Even after Dunkirk, God was thanked for having allowed so many Allies to get away, ignoring the converse of a God who had helped the Germans inflict on the British a complete rout.

As Deputy Chaplain General 21 Army Group Hughes wrote after D Day 1944 in the same vein, that greater efforts to consecrate a Force can never have been made. The King and his High Command believed in the supremacy of God, acknowledged the issue of war to be His, asked His aid, and wished his troops to be brought to God and taught the Christian way. They set out knowing that the work of Liberation was God's Will and an expressed purpose of Christ. All along they had been reminded that they carried God's Standards. These were sentiments prodigious in their presumption of Divine support of Allied arms.

In an address entitled 'The Consecration of our Armies' which he gave on the BBC Home Service 15th June 1944. He said

> As you think of them battling for the firm base across the Channel .... you will weigh my evidence as General Montgomery's chief padre, that many, many thousands of them went forth for righteousness sake, and for no other reason. They were not brought to battle by doctored propaganda. The chaplains were never asked to harness the Christian faith to military operations."

Asked to or not, Hughes, himself, gives evidence that he did, and in a manner reminiscent of the more extreme attitude of World War I chaplains. One is repeatedly reminded that Hughes, a subaltern in World War I, was regurgitating what he had heard and been impressed by from that time.

In a letter to his senior chaplain, Hughes (1943- 5 Aug) wrote

> C.... is in trouble with the Commanding Officer 31 Light Anti Aircraft Regiment and I must move him. The reason is that he took too light a view of his duty to inspire the unit when marked for Service abroad and joked about 'not wanting to go abroad'. This shook the Colonel's confidence and has been a root of mischief. It cannot be too plainly said that the Padre of all men

must be deadly serious that the Lord God Almighty on these occasions has called upon the Unit to do their stuff for Truth and Right and his trumpet must give no uncertain sound. I will put him in 6 Sub Area and ask him never again to laugh about the Call of God to the men of this Army.

The equivalence of a unit wartime posting with the call of the Lord God Almighty is breathtaking in its simplicity as well as providing evidence of a senior chaplain using his ministry to influence other chaplains to be better servants of the State. If, as Young and Wilson (1986:2) state, 'the task of ministry is enabling people to discern God', Hughes was Cromwellian in his presumption of God's support even for British army administration. Wilcock's reply (1943 Aug) "Yes, move C .... forthwith. Anyone who makes a joke of his calling should be 'shot at dawn' in the Eighth Army." is evidence that Hughes' attitude was not a singular aberration but, within the organization's thought forms, an unremarkable view.

To the question 'Has Religion grown in Eighth Army?' the reply given by Hughes (1943) is an exemplar of military religion legitimating the military enterprise.

Religion in Eighth Army is part of our fighting efficiency and has developed alongside all our other attainments .... The High Command gives Religion a primary place as decisive in war. We are led by faith in the inviolate supremacy of Almighty God .... He makes the fateful decision of national continuance or rejection and bends wars to His will. Therefore Eighth Army worships Him in humble duty.

According to Hughes, Montgomery's assertion that he would as soon think of going fighting without his artillery as without his chaplains, "gives chaplains full commission to try to bring the Army to the eve of battle consecrated as King Arthur's Knights of Chivalry." That there was no evidence of great Christian revival and sense of high endeavour, except in his own mind, did not inhibit Hughes, (1943) "This secret, sensitive feeling after God does not

wish to be talked about and is often shy of Services and Church."
That men were not permitted to be shy of Services and Church
through chaplaincy support of compulsory Church Parades, is now
addressed.

Church Parades

> January 7th 1917, Sunday. A great to-do was made of a
> Drumhead Service on our chateau lawn conducted by a
> bishop. Troops from the surroundings were brought
> over. Division and Brigade turned up in panoply and in
> force. It is said that a bishop once preached to a mere
> half-dozen voluntaries. He made such a fuss about the
> indignity, and waste of spiritual unction, that an Order
> from High Up required the attendance of 'the greatest
> possible number' on these solemn occasions: hence the
> crush. One can almost pardon the bishops their
> banalities since audiences were ordered for them.
> (Dunn, 1994, 289).

> One thing the common man cannot abide, and that is
> cant. And the churches to him are the embodiment of
> cant(Army and Religion 1919:229)

The Church of England chaplains fought a rearguard action until
1946 to retain what were known as Parade Services which were the
Army's version of the traditional English Sunday. The obligation
pressed less heavily upon Roman Catholic soldiers who were
expected by their church to attend Mass and to some degree expected
it of themselves. The vast majority of soldiers however, then as now,
resented formal religious functions and the compulsory Church
Parade did much to rob any well-thought-of chaplain of whatever
kindly feelings soldiers might have harboured for him. Studdert
Kennedy (1919:89) failed to appreciate the ironic contradiction in his
words that heretics were no longer burned nor even compelled to
worship in any special way. Religious freedom had been attained
"We would not do what God will never do: drive men to worship and
obey."

The Army compelled the soldier to do both. The chaplain was clearly seen to have a vested interest in what was a heartily detested practice and justly suffered the opprobrium of his association with the retention of one of the more repellent features of the military system. (Smyth 1968:271) records that the Canadians and the New Zealanders came down in favour of compulsory Church Parades and maintained that in war time there were powerful arguments in favour of that decision, but noticably fails to record a single one. Their converging views can be explained by the fact that in two very similar bodies, the same religious and military organizational pressures which influenced those who argued for its retention in England were at work in the Chaplaincies of other armies of Empire. To argue that because church attendance in the country was greater then than now so there would have been less resentment over compulsory Church attendance in the army is simply not borne out by the evidence.

Bishop Taylor Smith had earlier opposed the abolition of Church Parade on the grounds that many of the men who joined the Army were of such an age that they needed the strongest advice that could be given on moral and spiritual matters. Strictly utilitarian in his approach to religion he concluded

> That the Army used the occasion as an inspection parade..... did not in itself constitute sufficient reason for depriving the men of a chance of listening to useful sound advice which would mean considerable gain to the man himself if it was followed and would add to the efficiency of the Army as a whole. (Whitlow 1938:93-94)

In the judgement of a chaplain in 1926 the abolition of compulsory Church Parades would immensely weaken discipline and "The voluntary system would inevitably lead to the most undesirable denominational competition" (Bull 1926:Jan 185). The argument in effect was only to postpone the day when the Established Church would have to face the truth that without the element of compulsion, their proportion of Sunday worshipper's compared to nominal strength was very small. In fact it was already known in 1918 in France:

> March 31st Easter Day. Blue sky and sunshine, grand
> black and white cloud effects...... Civilians filled the
> parish church to the doors for morning service. In the
> afternoon they sat out of doors gossiping and drinking
> beer. Our voluntary services did not draw one
> worshipper among them all, to the padres' unholy
> indignation. (Dunn, 1994, 460).

From a sermon entitled "The Place of the Church in the Life of the Army", preached at Cambridge on October 21, 1928, by the Chaplain General the Reverend A C E Jarvis, it can be learned how one man at a precise time viewed both compulsory Church Parades and the Role of the Chaplains' Department. Jarvis stated that every man coming into the army was brought under 'immediate spiritual influence' and amongst other things to go to Church. The reason for compulsion he claimed was that it was impossible to conceive of any well ordered life recognising the claims of authority and discipline without religion. He concluded "So rightly conceived, the Chaplains' Department of the Army is a great Missionary agency of the Church". To what degree this was the Church of England in the person of the Chaplain General 'whistling past the cemetery', aware of massive defection but putting a brave face on it, is difficult to determine, though as early as the Boer War, chaplains had noted how little the serviceman was influenced by Christianity. That discovery, selectively forgotten, was matched by a West Point chaplain in 1908, William J Roe, claiming that their 'best endeavours failed utterly to produce any change whatever in the attitude of the cadets towards orthodoxy'. (Stover 1977:239)

When the 'Radio Padre' was asked should Church Parades be compulsory he likened it to Physical Training which was compulsory and appealed to the fact that the great soldiers, sailors and airmen had been churchgoers, who put religion in its right place. The special pleading and singular use of a scripture text are an object lesson in dysfunctional ministry and deserve to be quoted in full.

And even if all these reasons don't mean a thing to you, and I should be sorry if some of them didn't, we have our Lord's instruction "Go out into the highways and byways and make them come in." You see the Army is part of the Forces of the Crown and the King is King of a country which holds that the service of God is the most important part of life - which is the big reason (incidentally) why we're at war with Hitler who given his own way wouldn't allow you to be a Christian. Church Parade is part of the whole corporate life of your regiment, as part of 'service' in a very real sense and that is on a higher plane than cleaning brasses and the rest. I know that all the real good soldiers I've met will agree with me on this. (Wright 1943:31)

If not intentionally dishonest, such advocacy even to the final line casting those who do not agree out of the company of 'real good soldiers' can have done nothing to enhance the probity of chaplains. It would be interesting to discover whether the following, written by C. S. Lewis, was engendered by his antipathy to the cant of Ronald Selby Wright the radio padre.

"I have even heard …. defend compulsory games on the ground that all boys 'except a few rotters' like the games; they have to be compulsory because no compulsion is needed. (I wish I had never heard chaplains in the Armed Forces produce a similar argument in defence of the wicked institution of Church Parades.)" (Lewis 1959:189)

Freddie Hughes who was successful in achieving within the Army a high profile for chaplaincy, when he became Chaplain General, failed in his attempt to retain compulsory attendance at church. Even with Montgomery's backing, the social changes that were already taking place in post war Britain made its retention impossible. The decision was taken to make Church attendance optional except for special occasions and by 1992 attendance even at Remembrance Sunday services is only encouraged not enforced.

Though chaplains are quite unable to enforce church attendance on anyone some Regimental Commanding Officers still bring illegitimate pressure to bear upon their soldiers to attend Company or Squadron services. Regimental or Company pride brings peer pressure to enforce conformity with the result that those who might refuse or resent such pressure to engage in religious worship are encouraged to see it merely as a distasteful duty which must be accepted for the good of the group. Though it ceases to have anything to do with meaningful religious worship, many chaplains still connive at it.

Padre McLusky, who served with the Special Air Service in France, gives an insight into what worship can be for soldiers. He said that they did not worship because they were afraid. Worship had meaning and reality for them because they lived together and they shared the same hopes and fears. In contrast, those who lived round an English parish church only happened to live together. In their 'togetherness' there was no community. If they were so little 'one' throughout the week it was unsurprising that they failed to be 'one' on Sunday. A further reason which made their worship seem natural and meaningful was that they worshipped where they lived. In the clearing where they slept or round a fire which was home, worship was part of their daily life. This conjunction of religion and life in wartime is rarely documented and does not seem to have been used, at least in the instance recounted above, as overt legitimation of the military enterprise. It was, it seems, a genuine 'koinonia'.

The available documentary evidence supports the thesis that chaplains by a process of explanation and justification in both World Wars supported the aims and interests of the army. It is not necessary to assume that this was specifically their objective - though for many it might have been - nor that the chaplains were even conscious of it. The transition from religion in the army to army religion happened regardless of the intention of the chaplain. As religion is such a potent force for social control, the use made of it in wartime was all the more intense because of its link to the sacred. When Studdert Kennedy or Freddy Hughes or Padre X 'baptised' the whole endeavour, with talk of Divine support, deviance from that group norm would only be for the bravest. Most did not deem opposition worthwhile. "Gott mit uns" had become Anglicised.

The following chapter is an analysis of the written replies of British Army chaplains who had served in the Gulf War in 1991 to a questionnaire sent to them on their return. The rationale behind the inclusion of such evidence follows from the belief that in offering an explanation of a social phenomenon, it is important to discover how it is seen from the viewpoint of the participants.

Chapter 5

Vietnam and Gulf Chaplains' Questionnaire

Methodology

Only a fool would contend that military chaplains as those most consistently responsible for interpreting the biblical faith to the military could have prevented our nation's assault on Vietnam or even its symbolic apogee in the murders at My Lai. The undeniable fact is that our military forces were sent into Vietnam by civilian strategists and commanders who, however they may have been influenced by military advice, still bear the responsibility for having taken the decision. The other sad fact is that on the question of Vietnam, the whole religious community failed, and failed miserably. It failed in both its historic responsibilities vis-à-vis war. First it failed to warn us that there were no compelling moral reasons to **get into** the war (in fact the moral arguments clearly indicated the opposite). And then it failed to restrain the means utilised once the decision to wage war was made. In Vietnam we have watched aghast as our side devastated villages ("to save them"), forcibly moved civilian populations, poisoned croplands with chemical pesticides and transformed a lovely nation into a charred ruin. Who was speaking out for the ancient moral principle of "proportionate means" during all this? Almost no one. Consequently an examination of the chaplaincy must proceed only within a larger and more comprehensive questioning of why the whole American religious community failed so utterly to perform its religious and moral task.

(Cox, 1971,vi)

The project envisaged for this dissertation was an attempted replication of the findings of the study by Henry F Ackerman published in 1989 entitled *He Was Always There : The US Army Chaplain Ministry in the Vietnam Conflict.* The comparison was between the findings reported there and Role of British Army Chaplains in the Gulf War 1991.

The methodology used by Ackerman in writing what he describes as "this history" was fourfold:

i.   research of existing literature on the Vietnam war.
ii.   extensive taped interviews with 40 selected Vietnam chaplain veterans.
iii.   a survey questionnaire of 1350 Vietnam combat chaplains.
iv.   a survey questionnaire of 2200 Vietnam combatants, officers and servicemen.

The Ackerman study took more than five years to complete. A decision was made to restrict my questionnaire solely to the chaplains themselves and concentrate on how the chaplain saw his own role. It soon became obvious that history had determined that there would be serious methodological flaws in attempting too close a comparison between a military chaplaincy which lasted in Vietnam from 3 March 1962, when the first chaplain arrived there, to the departure of the last on 28 March 1974 and the ministry of British Army Chaplains, most of whom spent less than five months in the Gulf , and though under sporadic air attack, endured a war which lasted a spectacular few days. The limitation of parts of this study to the level of descriptive analysis is largely determined by the discovery made through conversations with some of the chaplains that the questionnaire sent to them for this research was the third they had received in addition to any official report they were asked to write. This went some way to explain the brevity of some of the replies and the comparative reluctance to enlarge upon answers given.

The only alteration in the Ackerman questionnaire to that sent to the British Chaplains was the substitution of the word Vietnam for Gulf. Sent to all 34 British Army Chaplains who served in the Gulf, the response to the questionnaire of 28 was very high, 82% compared with the 51% return in the Ackerman study, though in the latter it ensured more than six hundred replies. It should be stated that of the 28 replies, one was to say that he had not come to terms with his Gulf experience therefore could not complete the questionnaire. A second mostly answered his own questions and concluded 'In truth I can't really fit my ministry in to your great plan. Please believe me I am not trying to be awkward for once but I can't really see my role within your agenda.' A third treated the questionnaire very suspiciously, answered many questions with the words 'not prepared to answer at this point' and was the only one not to authorise the publication of the information he gave other than the numerical data his reply provided.

Comparative Analysis

Of the twenty-eight chaplains who replied, the youngest was 27 and the oldest was 52. Though there must be some hesitation in comparing features of US Army Chaplaincy between 30 and 18 years ago with present day British Army Chaplaincy, the average age of those in any rank was higher in 1991 than the US chaplains in the comparable rank in Vietnam. A tentative explanation could be the relatively recent phenomenon of later age entry into the Chaplains' Department. The figures are as follows:

Total	Ranking as Chaplain	British Average Age	US Average Age
19	4th Class (Captain)	35	34
6	3rd Class (Major)	44	39
3	2nd Class (Lt Col)	49	46

The first three questions were concerned with an evaluation of chaplaincy training, military training and university or seminary training, using the scale A to I

Very Good			Fair			Very Poor		
A	B	C	D	E	F	G	H	I

88

1. Chaplaincy training was rated	ABC by 44%	(US 54%)
	DEF by 48%	(US 38%)
	GHI by 8%	(US 8%)
2. Military training was rated	ABC by 64%	(US 69%)
	DEF by 32%	(US 29%)
	GHI by 4%	(US 2%)
3. Civilian Education and Training	ABC by 81%	(US 78%)
	DEF by 15%	(US 20%)
	GHI by 4%	(US 2%)

Chaplaincy training was evaluated appreciably lower by the British chaplains. This was borne out by a specific comment made by one chaplain in his report, who said that

> Training needed review. On joining the Department there were six weeks introductory training. The four weeks at the Royal Military Academy (Sandhurst) was of little use to chaplains save for the experience it provided of what a platoon commander might do. Surely there is a place for a more related training programme : something more specialized concentrating on the role of the chaplain

Others made similar comments, although the above appeal has repeatedly been made by chaplains over the years since World War II, the Department's failure to comply cannot simply be due to Departmental indecision. This study has shown that the wide range of activities engaged in by chaplains would be impossible to train for. One chaplain, a Bisley prizewinner, on the way to the Falklands, instructed soldiers in weapon firing - an activity which other chaplains might have considered to be grounds for resigning his chaplaincy. If anyone in authority, of any persuasion, were sufficiently bold to say *this* is the chaplain's role, and defined it any more precisely than expressed in the Chaplains' Handbook, others would feel free to disagree. The imprecision of the role is looked upon by some as a strength while others see in it weakness. Russell's reference (1980:270) to clergy self image as 'independent professional men' who themselves decide what is their role, is a measure of the growing imprecision of their claim to professionalism in the sense that lawyers or medical men make that claim. Of course not all would claim the epithet professional.

Of the categories which were to be put in rank order as having done most to prepare a chaplain for war service in the Gulf/Vietnam

BRITISH		US
3rd	Chaplain Training	2nd
1st	Military Training	2nd
3rd	Seminary/University Training	5th
2nd	Prior experience as clergyman	4th
5th	Common sense	1st

the dissimilarity between the responses - the US chaplains rated common sense first and the British 5th - is remarkable and difficult to interpret. The US study concluded that if common sense was so highly rated it was a commodity which could not be trained for. That the Gulf Study rated it last might imply that in a desert war common sense counted for very little, whereas prior military training and Ministerial experience were more important.

To the fifth question whether the training of a chaplain for possible combat situations should be changed, only 17 out of 26 chaplains responded, but 65% of those said it should be changed compared to the 74% in the US survey. The lessons learned under combat conditions might naturally result in an appeal for a change in training for chaplaincy. This has to be balanced by the finding that the British chaplains considered their military training as having done most to prepare them for Gulf service. This might sound like a truism but training has often prepared armies to fight the last war, not the one currently engaged in and there is a sense in which this will always be so. The findings seem to show far greater satisfaction with military as opposed to chaplaincy training.

The most substantial portion of the questionnaire asked the chaplain to assess his relationship with those with whom he worked. The categories used in questions 6 - 20 were

Friendly	Neutral
Supportive	Hostile
Helpful	Other (please explain)
Businesslike	

As in the US study, the overwhelming preponderance of ticks were against the words 'Friendly,' 'Supportive' and 'Helpful' which would indicate that the relationship between the chaplain and other Army members was a positive one. Chaplains who worked in Field Hospitals were notably critical of the leadership qualities of those who commanded these hospitals, implying that doctors had been promoted more for their medical skills than their leadership qualities. An added criticism of the medical profession was made more than once viz. the failure by many doctors to see a role in the medical arena for the chaplain. Though there was an acknowledgement of the role of the chaplain to Field Hospitals, in some Territorial Army (Reserve) Units there did not appear to be that awareness spoken of in the Vietnam survey.

> In the hospitals chaplains were part of the healing team offering soldiers holistic care that increased chances for rapid recovery. Many who worked with chaplains for the first time became aware of the chaplain as an important resource in the healing process. (Ackerman 1989:99)

The third section, questions 21-26, was concerned with Ministry.

Question 21 asked the chaplains to rank numerically ten aspects of ministry in the order of time spent doing them in the Gulf, marking 10 for the most time spent and 1 for the least time spent. The listing was as follows:

a. Sacramental
b. Counselling
c. Presence (visiting troops)
d. Visitation of Sick and Wounded
e. Worship Services

f.   Memorial Services
g.   Civic action
h.   Evangelism
i.   Corresponding with families of soldiers
j.   Others (please specify)

There was a very close similarity between the Vietnam and Gulf findings, the chaplains naming the same four categories in order of priority:

GULF	VIETNAM
Ministry of Presence	Ministry of Presence
Visitation of Sick and Wounded	Counselling
Worship	Visitation of Sick and Wounded
Counselling	Worship

Asked to rank the same list in the order of importance placed on them in the Gulf /Vietnam:

GULF	VIETNAM
Ministry of Presence	Ministry of Presence
Visitation of Sick and Wounded	Counselling
Worship	Visitation of Sick and Wounded
Counselling	Worship

Counselling took higher priority in Vietnam due to the extended nature of the war and the tension induced in combatants who knew of the anti-war lobby back home. The support by the UN of the Gulf intervention Forces seem to have absolved many combatants of the soul-searching engaged in by Vietnam troops.

Along with the Ackerman survey it can safely be said that as with the Vietnam chaplains so with those in the Gulf they spent most of their time performing what they considered to be the most important aspects of ministry.

One Gulf chaplain maintained that he spent 25% of his time in travel. The most frequent complaint made by chaplains was the initial lack of transport and the failure by the Army as a whole to appreciate that, without dedicated transport, the chaplain is rendered ineffective. Though in time chaplains obtained transport, the initial deprivation aggravated the problem faced by many chaplains of having to minister to troops spread over large areas.

In a letter dated 5th November 1990 one chaplain apropos having no transport wrote that he had to accept lifts from Squadron Quartermasters or take a Bedford Truck. "I spend my days humping stores around the A1 Eschelon driving Bedfords and visiting the Squadrons. I am happy and content and see lots of the boys." The Quartermaster's role was enforced in order to obtain transport rather than a preferred option.

Another chaplain wrote Tuesday 26 February 1991 that he had kept a little of his sanity by rewriting the computer system which recorded and reported casualties and that he was currently working on a system which analysed what happened in operating theatres with the aim of ensuring better treatment in the next war. The significance of what he wrote was that he was concerning himself with hospital procedures, which is strictly a hospital concern, not with chaplaincy procedures under which he himself had suffered and yet he saw more advantage in programming for better hospital procedures than facilitating the chaplaincy role. It is difficult to imagine any doctor in the same situation composing a computer programme better to assist the chaplain in his role.

Of descriptive words most illustrative of their ministry Gulf chaplains chose the same four categories as chosen by Vietnam chaplains. The categories were:

a.   Satisfied
b.   Overwhelmed
c.   Able to cope with whatever came up
d.   Adequate
e.   Properly utilized
f.   Underutilized
g.   Unsure
h.   Other feelings

'Satisfied', 'able to cope', 'adequate' and 'properly utilized' were the categories chosen by 82% of Gulf chaplains and 85% of Vietnam chaplains.

Question 24. Did the Gulf experience change your ministry? The possible answers were 'Yes', 'No', 'Unsure'. The Vietnam chaplains' responses were divided into those who replied with either a positive or negative change in the ministry. Hence the disparity:

GULF		VIETNAM
34%	No, Ministry unchanged	34%
38%	Yes, Ministry changed	61%
26%	Unsure	5%

There were few elaborations on the answers given in the Gulf survey. One chaplain 'presumed' that the experience had made him more mature. Another expressed a change towards a more sacramental ministry while a third stated 'I have come to recognize the work of the Holy Spirit in the lives of the most unlikely people.'

Question 25. Did the Gulf experience change your life in other ways? If so how?

GULF		VIETNAM
43%	No change	25%
57%	Change	72%
	Unsure	3%

Among comments made were -

... keener on disarmament. Appreciate the goodness of people.
... Forced reflection on one's own faith and one's own death.
... A greater appreciation of and love of life. It made me realise how much I loved my family.
... I left for the Gulf in December 90. In June 91 I was back in my office with the same people as before doing the same job as before, as if it had all been a dream. Not one soldier or officer from the Division had been killed.

Question 26. Were there any hindrances to your ministry while a chaplain in the Gulf? Please elaborate.

GULF		VIETNAM
48%	Yes	40%
52%	No	60%

As in the Vietnam survey the major hindrance by far in the Gulf was lack of transport at least initially. In a personal letter dated 12 January 91 one chaplain wrote:

... my Church of England oppo and myself were totally barred (at a very high level - a political decision) from leaving Bahrain not withstanding the fact that at the time there was no British service chaplain in the whole of Saudi and that part of my unit - was just an hours drive away at the edge of Saudi.

Roman Catholic chaplains were critical of the lack of support they received from their Principal Chaplain:

Bagshot (Ministry of Defence Chaplains) was also hopelessly too late in formalizing my appointment as Senior Chaplain Roman Catholic. The delay left a huge hole which is initially impossible to fill. Fortunately, relationships between all chaplains seem, by and large, excellent.

Anglican chaplains were appreciative of the support they received from their Senior Chaplains.

Question 27. Was your faith strengthened, weakened, unchanged, other?

GULF		VIETNAM
65%	Strengthened	82%
4%	Weakened	2%
19%	Unchanged	14%
12%	Other	2%

Though not as high as the figure in the Vietnam survey (96%) those who said their faith was strengthened or unchanged by the Gulf War was (84%), similar comments to the US survey were made that 'impending death concentrated the mind'

a) ... In the desert you have nothing ... all your possessions you carry ... The desert war heightens one's spiritual feelings. I have a tremendous sense of inward peace .... it feels like euphoria but I know it is not. It's like metal tested in the fire.

b) ... I became much more tolerant of and grateful for the diversity of the faith of others.

c) ... the power of world-wide prayer was felt constantly.

d) ... for the first time I became aware of my neglect towards my own thoughts on death/eternal life. I had to search long and hard into my own faith and how that affected me. I also had to come to terms with fear of my own death.

e) ... I found God as hard to trace in the Gulf as I do in the barracks.

f) ... I think that I came away from the whole experience with a heightened awareness of the meaning of the phrase 'the fellowship of believers' for there is no doubt that we are an increasingly small minority. This of course is simply a reflection of our society.

g) ... I was so regularly overwhelmed by work that I became more dependent on God each day.

One chaplain who said his faith was 'challenged' stated that "I needed to confront a) whose side was God on, b) did I really believe in personal resurrection if I died, c) how could I find time and energy to pray?"

Question 29 asked whether their attitude towards the military had changed as a result of their Gulf experience.

GULF		VIETNAM
62%	No change	65%
38%	Change	34%

One chaplain said he was shocked by the selfishness and personal ambition at others expense demonstrated by some senior officers as well as by the envy of those who did not go to the Gulf towards those who did. Most expressed admiration at the professionalism of the military. One complained of 'having to justify every decision with a three page document' even in the Gulf. Another did not think that the Army took chaplaincy very seriously despite all the official protestations about the importance of the role of the chaplain, but saw it as a reflection of the 'drastically reduced public influence of the church in society.'

A most dramatic accusation was made by one chaplain who stated 'I was angry because the hospital was sited on a military target in direct contravention of the Geneva Convention. I became a bit suspicious (of the integrity of the military).' He went on to state that his attitude both towards the military and the chaplaincy were changed for the worse as a result, since his complaint to the chaplaincy had received no response. 'I'm no longer overawed by the bullshit' is a summary of numerous chaplains' replies which are balanced by the assertion of another "We are a very professional army. As chaplains we must be equally professional."

The plea for greater professionalism links currently serving chaplains with Studdert Kennedy. Feigned or believed, there had been a quite prevalent attitude shown by some chaplains implying that chaplains should be above the sweating and grunting side of soldiery. Personal fitness and basic military knowledge were not taken seriously and as a consequence a number of chaplains posted to the Gulf were declared medically unfit to do so and could not go.

Question 30. Did your attitude towards the chaplaincy change as a result of the Gulf experience? How?

GULF		VIETNAM
54%	No change	64%
46%	Change	34%

In contrast to being the official 'caring' organisation, a number of chaplains noted the lack of debrief or counselling by the Chaplains' Department - the lack of post Gulf care that was shown. One chaplain 'became more aware of how ambitious some chaplains are for promotion' while another saw 'great pastoral gifts displayed and offered'.

Question 31. Did your attitude towards the civilian community change as a result of the Gulf experience? How?

GULF		VIETNAM
59%	No change	44%
41%	Change	55%
		(51% negative change)

One reply to the Vietnam survey reads "I became very frustrated and angry with liberal politicians and others who defeated us in Vietnam". (Ackerman 1989:231)

The difference between the outcome of Vietnam and the Gulf War could be expected to influence attitudes and patently did. Though not logically sound, the following expression was typical:

> The overwhelming support we received from the civilian community proves that the average citizen is in favour of the modern army.

Another spoke of the effect on morale of the tremendous lay and ecclesiastical support shown by letters and parcels. Annoyance was expressed that 'So many British civilians bask under the protection of our Services with no obvious appreciation of the cost involved to Service personnel and their families.'

The literally overwhelming amount of mail sent to one chaplain 'was in many respects a curse' creating feelings of obligation to reply. This was a phenomenon referred to by many chaplains who resorted to printing a standard letter and merely adding a postscript. The most strongly expressed reaction was "Anger at the media 'circus'; anger at the Peace Movement; anger at the short memory of the average Brit; anger at the German and other nations supplying illegally chemical weapons and technology to the Iraqis; anger at those who decry the victory because Saddam Hussein remains in power."

Question 32. Overall what problems were most brought to you by soldiers in the Gulf.

The problems are listed below with the frequency they appeared in the chaplains' responses:

Marriage/girlfriend problems	13
Fear of danger/death	9
Fear of killing	6
Fear of inability to cope	3

These relate to the Ackerman finding in Vietnam, though homesickness/separation/loneliness was a problem most frequently faced there (Ackerman 1989:232)

Question 33. Overall what problems were most brought to you by officers in the Gulf?

Fear of inadequacy	5
Fear of inability to cope well	4
The morality of the war	4
Spiritual problem	3
Marriage/relationship problems	2
Separation	2

As in the US survey, a common view was that 'officers don't admit to problems' and that few shared theirs with the chaplain. One said it tended to be committed Christians who discussed their problems with the chaplain while another said that all problems revolve around fear.

It is worthwhile to note here that a number of chaplains in the Gulf reported that senior officers displayed a lack of knowledge as to the role of a chaplain and yet coupled with this is the repeated experience of having very senior officers requested to address chaplains at training conferences to give their view on the role of the chaplain. It is unsurprising that Generals put a premium on the pastoral role of chaplains which at its extreme replaces or dislodges the priority of God and his purposes. Pastoral care is increasingly offered by counsellors and social workers in a purely secular way. Though counselling, social work, pastoral care and administration are all functions which have devolved upon the chaplain, a military chaplaincy, unless it is grounded in God, primarily concerned with fostering a sense of God's reality in the whole of life - war included - is in repeated danger of being reduced to something less than itself.

Summary

With few notable exceptions there was a very close correlation between the results of the Ackerman Report and the Survey carried out on Gulf chaplaincy in the British Army, though attention should be drawn to the fact that there could be no close comparison between a chaplaincy covering a twelve year war and one in which the whole operation from first deployment to withdrawal was less than six months. Ackerman's findings relate to chaplaincy as experienced in a prolonged war as compared with the British Army chaplaincy survey, 99% of whose chaplaincy was preparation for war. Its significance might lie in it being a record of advance-to-war-chaplaincy which in many accounts is quickly passed over in favour of description of war itself.

Though apparently showing a concentration on those core functions which are said to be the irreducible core of his role, there was also evidence of chaplains who appeared dissatisfied with those defining functions, opting for a more visible 'practical role'

At .... upon my request I received further first-aid training and I was allocated a position with the evacuation team. This included being trained to monitor life-support systems. The staff gave every possible assistance, ensuring that my contribution was of an integral and necessary nature.

"They would wouldn't they", especially in the light of what another chaplain wrote

Among the Command Hierarchy within the Field Hospital there was at the outset limited understanding of the role of the Hospital chaplains other than as social workers and Sunday Service takers.

Once more, where the chaplain was prepared to relinquish his core role his offer to be 'useful' was not spurned. That other chaplains called for more first-aid training 'to enable chaplains to have a dual role' emphasises the abiding perception of the primary role as insufficient.

The ministry of 'presence', of being there, was significantly considered by both Vietnam and Gulf chaplains as the most important aspect of their ministry. Though from the Ackerman Report (1987:149) it is well illustrated by - 'a first sergeant showed one photo of me conducting a service in the field. He was of another faith but on the back he wrote "This is my chaplain - he is always with us." Those are the finest words ever said about my years in Vietnam.' The presence of the chaplain - being there - was in the opinion of one US chaplain a more potent reminder to the men of the reality of God's love for them than the most eloquent of sermons.

This study has concentrated upon the tensions and conflicts experienced by chaplains in their ministry especially in a wartime environment. That all chaplains were not successful in resisting pressures to support military objectives has been documented as has the fact that religion was used in support of secular aims. In answer to my written expression of surprise that in the Ackerman Survey there was a complete lack of reference to chaplaincy weaknesses or individual failure, Dr Hourihan, the US Chaplains' Branch historian, replied that my observation on the absence of critical material was correct but stated that it had to be remembered that Ackerman was on active duty at the time he wrote it and that the volume was an 'official' history. Hourihan concluded that from his own review of some of the material contained in the thirteen boxes of research data, he himself had a sense that a more critical history could have been written.

This almost incidental piece of data contained in personal correspondence is probably the most significant single finding of this study. It reinforces that observation, so often denied by those who would maintain the role of army chaplain to be a straightforward ministry but to a specialized group, that organizational and situational pressure consequent upon identification with and dependence upon significant groups (Army and Church) can and does produce demonstrative alterations in perception and behaviour. Because he was a serving chaplain writing an official history, Ackerman, if not consciously and deliberately, nonetheless did omit any evidence that might have reflected badly upon individual chaplains or the chaplaincy. Repeated readings of the Survey reinforces the suspicion that it is as hagiographical as it is a sociological work. A statement worthy of analysis made in 1968 by the Chief of Chaplains is accepted without comment

> The chaplain goes with them not as a hawk or a dove -
> but under the aegis of the American Eagle and in the
> inspiration of the Holy Paraclete. We too are soldiers -
> soldiers of America and - soldiers of God. (Ackermann
> 1989:15)

Concentration on a plethora of ministries; initiatives in combatting drug abuse; support of local churches; all are highlighted as activities evoking a natural pride, but of the question of the very involvement of the US in Vietnam, the atrocities of My Lai, Search and Destroy operations, forcible removal of civilian populations or the use of chemical pesticides and defoliants and other questionable activities upon which one might have expected chaplains to have had opinions, no mention is made.

Such selective compartmentalization cannot but remind one of the quixotic attitude of First World War chaplains whose crusades against swearing, drinking and sexual promiscuity had such little effect.

> February 2nd 1917... The Chaplain's tent was next to a Canteen from which he heard such frequent mention of 'f---ing biscuits' that he asked, and got his C.O. to make the sergeant post a sentry over the tin. 'to see that the biscuits committed no indecency.' (Dunn, 1994, 294).

Though here showing a sense of humour, such censure was subsequently seen as a classic example of displaced aggression whose obvious target deserving of condemnation was the pointless slaughter of the war itself. Similarly after the Second World War RAF chaplains were unwilling to condemn the use of atomic weapons against civilian populations but would state categorically that they would oppose, if it were proposed, the opening of a Station brothel. The expectation that RAF chaplains would have familiarized themselves with the implications of the saturation bombing of Dresden or have considered what advice they might give as to its moral implications might have been presumed. It was considered to be one of the most important findings of the study by Zahn (1969:165) "that anyone who would make either or both of those assumptions would be quite wrong."

In the Gulf survey a strong impression is given by the chaplains of an overall feeling of the self-evident rightness of the war against Iraq. As in World War I when it was reported that after the Armistice two chaplains were overheard to complain that insufficient towns had been flattened and the latest gas had not been given a fair run, so there was a guilty admission by some Gulf chaplains of feeling cheated at the brevity of the war. It has to be stated that in their enlarged reports, though chaplains made reference to counselling soldiers over some spectacular horror of war, no attempt was made by the chaplains to identify themselves with similar misgivings. For example one chaplain said he 'attempted' to counsel soldiers who had seen enemy forces being annihilated by artillery whilst apparently trying to surrender. Another wrote that there was a certain amount of guilt felt after the battle because on occasion the infantry, to whom he was chaplain, had to "open up" on surrendering Iraqis because enemy fire was coming in from behind them.

> Time after time I have heard fellow chaplains deride the idea of offering to pray with soldiers. My experience in the Gulf was that a few soldiers at the end of a conversation would ask me to pray for them or their family. However whenever I suggested to anyone that I pray with them, their response was immediate and positive. If the Royal Army Chaplaincy Department cannot pray with those in its care, who can? We need to be bold in offering to pray with people notwithstanding our own natural diffidence or feelings of unworthiness.

So wrote a Gulf chaplain and it is difficult to dissent from the finding of Zahn that many clergymen too readily reconcile themselves to having to sacrifice some of their 'spirituality' when they join the Army chaplaincy and that they may have to go along with some things of which they would not ordinarily approve. If chaplains feel unable or are unwilling to make effective protest in the face of apparent wrongdoing, one is forced to ask with Zahn whether the military dimension of the chaplain's role is of as little influence on their behaviour as they apparently and sincerely believe. The evidence forces the conclusion that the prophetic ministry of chaplains is thereby subverted and that unreflective chaplains give no evidence of awareness even of the problem. Evidence of the application of theology by chaplains to their role is disturbingly absent, due it would seem to the presumption of the rightness of their presence with the military, an attitude showing little appreciation of even possible moral ambiguity. What is apparent is an attitude, unbroken since World War One, of demonstrating a simple unreflective alignment of Christianity and war together with an absence of creative dissent towards the institution chaplains serve.

Chapter 6

Contemporary Army Chaplaincy

Myths and Stereotypes

The respect in which the British Forces is held by society is due largely to its social legitimation as an institution of the Crown. The Queen remains the titular head of the army in whose name Commissions, Warrants and Regulations are issued. There is an extent to which society has mythologised the military profession, seeing it as the selfless service and unlimited liability of those prepared to die in defence of their country. In spite of the fact that in modern warfare as many civilians are killed as military, that myth remains. Army chaplaincy shares in the myth which chaplains do nothing to dispel, apparently unconcerned by stereotyped images of their role.

One such stereotype already considered is the "collared warhawk in the aviary" (Cox, 1971:60). It is not a preferred image which myth would have us believe died in Flanders, but evidence proves its survival to the present. In a letter dated 11 February 1991, a Roman Catholic chaplain in Saudi Arabia referred to 'one divide', which, he wrote, marked him out from his 'Separated Brethren'. He said 'they' seemed quite at home preaching Christ as some formidable American trouble-shooter, who would lead them all to victory and have the desert scorpions, rats and foxes running off to their holes to Onward Christian Soldiers, Soldiers of Christ Arise and Stand up, stand up for Jesus. Hesitation in accepting such a pejorative assessment by one chaplain of his colleagues, especially when it is known how extensive were the areas chaplains were expected to cover, is lessened by two factors. Firstly, many Gulf chaplains wrote in their reports of working alongside one another, often across denominational barriers, preaching at one another's services. Secondly, and in the light of the finding of this study, more significantly, the chaplain quoted was one who had served little more than two years and has since left, who had notably resisted that incorporation by which year by year, chaplains who serve longer are absorbed by the organization and assimilate its world-view.

A preferred stereotype is the chaplain as man of God, preferably tough; the priest, the padre, completely dedicated, who shares every trial, and danger with the men and receives in return their deep and undying gratitude. This image owes much to the idealised role stemming from World War One, which biography, film and television has uncritically perpetuated. The reality is far more mundane, ambivalent and ultimately human. In one instance, the heroic stereotype has led a Methodist chaplain into gross misrepresentation:

> The army demands a lot of its chaplains...... answers to
> its welfare problems .... pastoral cover .... coping with
> situations in the field, sporting activities, adventure
> training, Mess functions .... standing in for officers who
> are sick. I am paid twenty four hours a day, seven days
> a week and they have the right to expect I am worthy of
> my hire. (McLeish, 1990:7)

The content of this Stakhanovite testament does not bear analysis. The vast majority of welfare problems are dealt with by professional welfare agencies. Chaplains do not stand in for sick officers, any more than laymen stand in for sick chaplains. The inclusion of cocktail parties, Mess receptions and Regimental dinners or adventure training and sport, as chaplain specific, in what purports to be a job description is seen as the attempt by one army chaplain, so unsure of what constitutes ministry, to conclude that everything does. It is possible that all one does is done for God's greater glory, but this in no way is exclusive to religious ministers.

The most glaring omission from the preferred stereotype of the chaplain is his obvious humanity. He is ambitious, elitist and class conscious. That present day army chaplains from very ordinary backgrounds have children at major public schools is indicative also of substantial remuneration and educational grants. The chaplain is hypocritical, lazy and selfish in the same measure as his civilian counterparts and the rest of humanity. The difference is that within the Army these characteristics are fuelled and exaggerated and can be expected to militate against effective religious influence or leadership the more the chaplain becomes indistinguishable from his fellow officers.

Rank : Asset and Liability

The clergy not wanting to look the part has something to do with the dismantling of the Book of Common Prayer. Anxious not to sound like parsons they can hardly be blamed for not wanting to look like them either. The "underneath this cassock I am a man like any other act" must be a familiar routine at many a church door. Priests have always hankered after the world or at any rate the worldly and consorting as He did with publicans and sinners it was Jesus who started the rot. (Bennett, 1991,11)

The psychological benefit of group membership, conferred by the wearing of military uniform is as frequently as it is favourably commented upon by chaplains. The impression that it is a notable boost to religious ministry, is illusory on closer analysis and can be seen to embody a concern, as much with the advantage accruing to the chaplain, by his personal membership of the military, as the better to bring religion to the soldier. It is this latter which is assumed to be happening, but analysis highlights a preoccupation with acceptance whose benefits are chaplain, rather than soldier-orientated. By the dual significance of uniform and rank the chaplain can forget marginalization, so frequently experienced by his peers in contemporary society. Army chaplaincy is ministry from a basis of associational significance; ministry from a basis of power not weakness. Though only twenty may attend Regimental Sunday Service, the chaplain can assure himself of essential significance by uniform, rank, status and salary. Vivid confirmation was provided by a former chaplain, colonel equivalent recently retired, who exhorted me to 'Stay in as long as you can: outside you are nobody.' The import of such advice lies in the knowledge that when serving as a chaplain, the man was often heard to expatiate upon rank as having no meaning to chaplains, least of all to him. Chaplains nurture one another's delusions about the role and significance of rank. There is scant written evidence supporting the favoured assertion that soldiers felt close to the chaplain, even in wartime.

> March 19th, 1918. We'll win in the long run if the home front hold. The poisonous atmosphere there is disheartening….. In quests for a scheme of 'rededication' I can't help. I doubt if the men out here are more drawn to religion; I'm sure they are more than ever repelled by the clergy. (Dunn, 1994, 453)

Of course there were exceptions, but whatever comfort was taken from his presence, could be interpreted as much from reassurance provided by association with the mystical or magical, imagined, protective nature of religion, as any interpersonal link. Those chaplains who say that the wearing of uniform helps them get alongside the soldier might be correct, but they choose to ignore or suppress one element which the documentary evidence, as well as my own twenty years of personal experience cannot dispel: distancing is built into the system by means of badges of rank, which constrains chaplains to relate to soldiers as officers to other ranks, as superiors to inferiors. The mechanism of rank, retained by armies because of its undoubted efficacy, functions irrespective of the intention or belief of the chaplain that in his case, it should not; irrespective of the repeated assertion that chaplains are different from all other officers. This study has discovered no evidence to support the belief that those dislocating mechanisms of rank, accepted by all as defining everyone's position within the army structure and intended precisely to locate them, are suspended when applied to chaplains, though generations of chaplains have chosen to believe, and continue to prefer to believe, that they are. That they see a priest as a priest if he acts as a priest, regardless of his rank, is a simplistic uni-dimensional view of army chaplaincy which must be rejected as superficial and inadequate, in spite of the support given to this view by the Chaplains' Handbook.

Incremental verification is provided by the experience of many chaplains that badges of rank alter interpersonal relationships between chaplains, let alone between soldier and chaplain. All members of the army are conditioned instantly to recognise rank up and down, and react to it. It is not suspended for anyone and thus produces an area of tension or conflict which makes effective ministry difficult. Though it might have to be conceded that the wearing of uniform and even rank by chaplains seems historically to work best, such a submission need not force the corollary that a best-option necessarily excludes dysfunctional elements. It is the denial of the existence of unintended consequences of the wearing of rank by chaplains that has led to the failure by the Chaplains' Department to admit to the existence of a conflict, though the suggestion by it that, on occasion, the chaplain might wear clerical dress, is tacit admission of the potential for uniform in some situations to be counterproductive. The army operates by means of a rigid power structure in which the chaplains have chosen to share, but to what extent such a ministry reflects a Christlike mode, is open to question as is any success in remaining uninfluenced by the army's traditional system based on defining people by rank order. Though unacknowledged, rank remains a major source of insecurity for many chaplains. Berger sums it up perfectly with an example:

> A man recently commissioned as an officer, especially if he came up through the ranks, will at first be at least slightly embarrassed by the salutes he now receives from the enlisted men he meets on his way. Probably he will respond to them in a friendly, almost apologetic manner. The new insignia on his uniform are at that point still something he has merely put on, almost like a disguise. Indeed, the new officer may even tell himself and others that underneath he is still the same person, that he simply has new responsibilities (among which *en passant*, is the duty to accept the salutes of enlisted men). This attitude is not likely to last very long. In order to carry out his new role of officer, our man must maintain a certain bearing. This bearing has quite definite implications. Despite all the double-talk in this area that is customary in so-called democratic armies, such as the American one, one of the

fundamental implications is that an officer is a superior somebody, entitled to obedience and respect on the basis of this superiority. Every military salute given by an inferior in rank is an act of obeisance received as a matter of course by the one who returns it. Thus with every salute given and accepted (along, of course, with a hundred other ceremonial acts that enhance his new status) our man is fortified in his new bearing - and in its, as it were, ontological presuppositions .... He has become an officer almost as effortlessly as he grew into a person with blue eyes, brown hair, and a height of six feet .... Even very intelligent people, when faced with doubt about their roles in society, will involve themselves even more in the doubted activity, rather than withdraw into reflection ... Each role has its inner discipline, what Catholic monastics would call its 'formation'. The role forms, shapes, patterns both action and actor. It is very difficult to pretend in this world. Normally, one becomes what one plays at. (Berger, 1963, 113-115)

Rank Based Church Attendance

Research evidence provided by the Institute for American Church Growth, shows that churches grow, and grow best, where members have many characteristics in common and feel that they belong, by sharing similar interests and culture. In the context of the British Army those chaplains who are the main beneficiaries, supposing such factors to be operative, are Scottish Presbyterian ministers when chaplain to Scottish regiments. The perception of belonging, in such regiments, is given both to officers and soldiers by their shared national and cultural background, strong regimental traditions and a heritage in which the regimental Kirk shares. The occasional attendance of a Scottish soldier at the Kirk can provide a cohesive function not given by the attendance of an equivalent English regimental soldier at a Church of England army church. It is worth repeating in this context that attendance at the regimental Kirk, even for many officers, is fuelled as much by regimental as religious considerations. Such an assertion is based upon the observation of total non-attendance by the majority of such officers, when posted away from the regiment. Integration and a sense of identity is conveyed to the soldier by membership of the army itself. Church attendance in the English context singles out a particular soldier creating tension by distancing him from his peers, from his kind of people, so it is largely avoided.

It is incontrovertible that within army churches the majority of worshippers are officers and senior non-commissioned officers and their families. The Church is a context in which the chaplain feels at home, without appreciating the advantage and confidence given to him by familiar territory. The congregations in the army, drawn as they are from an organization in which everyone knows his place and keeps it, predict their future composition. Soldiers are conditioned against feeling at ease with superior officers. Living accommodation, eating facilities and other amenities are hierarchically segregated, reinforcing that distancing process. In spite of all the contraindications it is assumed by chaplains, as if self-evident, that soldiers will automatically feel at home in army churches, simply because the context and locus is religious, and that they would be welcomed by the chaplain if they were to attend. The fundamental equality of all before God is a way of thinking of no concern to the army, preached, of course, by the chaplain, but manifestly without practical consequences. The almost total absence of private soldiers from public worship in army churches, occasioned by whatever other factors, in the light of the above perceptions, can be seen to be a self-fulfilling prophecy.

Brief-Span Ministry

The length of time a chaplain is appointed to minister in a particular location, is stated in his Posting Order which includes the proviso, 'or according to the exigencies of the Service'. Postings, as they are called, last two years on average. My own postings are not untypical over a fourteen year period. Four two-year postings interspersed by five postings lasting eight, eleven, thirteen, fifteen and nineteen months. Such abbreviated ministries create both in the chaplain and successive congregations a mentality, if not an expectancy, of impermanence. Such a double impedance to the establishment of church community tends to reduce commitment, prevents the creation of close relationships and virtually guarantees that long term plans are not contemplated, still less developed. Some would argue that such two-year appointments are less disruptive in an army context than they would be in a civilian church, by reason that members of the army congregations are aware that they too will only be there for two years. Such a consideration compounds rather than resolves the problem. As the vowed permanence of a married relationship, being irrevocable, creates its own dynamic, so would a relationship in which neither party expected any permanence. Chaplaincy engagement to a particular church, which is predeterminately brief, must inevitably suffer from a rootlessness, affecting both minister and congregation, which predictably fails to produce a vibrant, growing religious community.

Not only is the practice of moving ministers every two years not followed by any mainstream church outside the army, for the reason that it is manifestly dysfunctional for effective ministry, but whatever advantages are perceived by those who continue the practice must primarily be in the interest of the army, since they are at variance with all accepted psychological and sociological recommendations concerning ministry as well as pastoral practice. The continuity provided by a regimental chaplain moving with the regiment is its own justification, but it is unclear what pastoral advantage is served by the rapid succession of chaplaincy moves, apart from organizational 'wisdom' that chaplaincy postings should parallel those of other officers in the army, whose careers are guided by the necessity of occupying a succession of positions, for a time sufficient to master their complexity, before moving on. As an operating principle for chaplaincy posting, there is no evidence that pastoral considerations are primary, providing yet another illustration of ecclesiastical considerations being subservient to military needs.

Minimal Lay Involvement

In the civilian community church growth is heavily dependent upon the input of lay men and women, accustomed to sharing responsibility for expansion, with the minister acting as catalyst. In the army, church members, unused to non-military modes of leadership suitable for voluntary associational activity, are often unable to relate to the chaplain unless in a hierarchical sense which coerces lay passivity. In the absence of church mission activity the chaplain spends time on the maintenance of existing chaplaincy structures and, without an evangelistic ministry outside the liturgical sphere, would be hard pressed to describe his precise occupational role.

Proclamation or Presence

The mere presence of the chaplain within the military structure is in practice accepted, if not even preferred, as sufficient Christian proclamation. It might legitimately be asked what benefit soldiers are supposed to derive from such a presence, especially when many chaplains are so reticent about mentioning God, except in a diffident, jocose manner to soldiers, as if 'Tommy does not want religion. I don't persuade him'. (Wilkinson, 1978:143) were the last word on the matter. With notable Free Church exceptions the proclamation of the Gospel in any evangelistic sense is engaged in, not by chaplains but by Army Scripture Readers, ex-servicemen and women whose official aim is 'to spread the saving knowledge of Christ among the personnel of HM Forces.' Though officially and publicly approved and commended, they are often privately derided by chaplains. A more rigorous analysis of what is occurring here would refine, rather than contradict, the conclusion that it is yet one more example of that reluctance shown by chaplains to become too involved in the specifically religious side of ministry, a disinclination discovered by this study.

> But doctrinally and therefore pastorally the ministry of the Church of England to the dying and bereaved was confused. 'Without some sort of doctrine of the communion of saints,' R.J. Campbell wrote in 1916, 'that Protestantism had little comfort to give to mourners for it has been so sadly silent regarding the fate of our dead.' (Wilkinson, 1978, 175).

The Gulf War Survey provided examples of unease expressed by chaplains on the matter of the dead and dying. One wrote that as he was from the evangelical wing of the church he had had little to do with the Last Rites etc. and was not too sure what to do. He was aware, he wrote, that the hospital staff expected him to do something (for the dead) and he would have liked to have been better prepared. Another chaplain declared himself ill-at-ease in the presence of dead soldiers, not knowing what to do and contenting himself with a brief prayer. Other Protestant chaplains had asked their High Church or Roman Catholic colleagues for hasty instruction on the theology and practice of Extreme Unction before the ground war started, without which they felt they had little to offer. Such apparent ineptitude might be surprising, as ministry to the dead and dying is not exclusively a wartime one, but two perceptions might temper a too critical judgement. Firstly, even in the army, death is still a great taboo subject, infecting even chaplains with a reluctance to confront it. Secondly, within the army, there are expectations accompanying the role of chaplain which direct his day to day activity and provide him with attitudes concerning how the chaplaincy role should be lived. The secular ethos within which a chaplain works influences him to a degree which can markedly decrease his interest in, and concern for, the specifically spiritual side of ministry, unless forced upon him in the confusion of war, where ambivalence and insecurity about core ministerial activity becomes apparent. It is understandable that such an assertion, supported by empirical data, does not readily obtain the concurrence of serving chaplains and for predictable reasons.

Role Conflict Revisited

> Remember it is your duty in common with the adjutant to report all the little scandals of the regiment to the commanding officer whose favour you should omit no means to court and procure. (Grose, 1787)

In 1995 public attention was drawn to the role of military chaplain after accusations were made during a Parliamentary Select

Committee Hearing alleging that a small number of chaplains in the Navy, Army and Air Force had broken their professional code of confidentiality. Assertion was made that unnamed chaplains, using information entrusted to them in confidence, had divulged the same to the military authorities which led to the interrogation and consequent dismissal from the Services of homosexuals who had confided in their chaplains. Whether homosexuals should be permitted to serve in the Armed Forces is not at issue here, but rather the significance of what was viewed as the misconduct of chaplains as informers for the military organization.

Before attempting an analysis of the mechanisms at work three points are worth making. First, accusations based on *post hoc ergo propter hoc* - after this, therefore on account of this - reasoning, may be erroneous. There is a logical fallacy in assuming that because Private A was interviewed by the Military Police after A's disclosure to the chaplain it must have been that the chaplain informed on A. He might or might not have done so.

Second, and highly significantly, though the allegations were called into question, no attempt was made to deny the charges either by the various Service Chaplaincies or by those who spoke for the Ministry of Defence. Predictably and with complete consistency, there was a strong reassertion by the leaders of the RAChD of the paramount obligation of chaplains to respect professional confidentiality. It was also strongly reemphasised that there was no expectation by the Army, still less an obligation imposed on chaplains, that they should report on the sexual tendencies of soldiers.

Third, cold comfort ought to be taken by chaplains from the small number of chaplains cited in the allegation. Supposing it is true that only a small percentage of those serving in the Armed Forces are homosexuals and supposing also that of these a yet smaller proportion had broached the vexed subject of their sexuality with a chaplain, a cogent argument might be made that the percentage of those chaplains confided in who betrayed that confidence, is alarmingly high.

Any chaplain who broke confidence almost certainly did not do so after sitting down and deliberating with himself where his balance of duty lay. "The strength of the process comes precisely from its unconscious, unreflecting character." (Berger 1963,114). The chaplain is simultaneously located in society as a clergyman and as an army officer. Fulfilling dual roles at such an intersection, certain control mechanisms designed to regulate behaviour in one role cut across those designed to regulate that in another. Ordination or status as a minister in an accredited Church is the requirement for acceptance as a chaplain within the military. On commissioning, military chaplaincy involves living and working within a compact group, e.g. the Army, in which a man is known and to which he is tied by feelings of personal loyalty because he is cared for, paid, promoted and achieves significance through that organization.

Although there is no reason why a chaplain, if so minded, could not speak out on the issue of homosexuality and the military, the likelihood of this happening is diminished for the reason given by Berger (1963,87) "very potent and simultaneously very subtle mechanisms of control are constantly brought to bear on the actual or potential deviant". The chaplain as a member of one of the mainstream Churches, belongs to a social structure which regulates the behaviour of its ministers. Tradition and training have furnished procedures through which conduct is channelled in a manner in which it appears that certain behaviour is the only one possible for an honourable clergyman. So, in the Churches stands the matter of confidentiality. In the ecclesiastical context, it has become an institutional imperative.

Role conflict is manifested when such confidentiality does not best serve the needs of the military service to which the chaplain belongs. In that context he is aware that homosexuality is currently seen as a factor disruptive of fraternity and efficient military operations, viewed with concern by the military authorities. Chaplains as a body, because they feel at home with dogmatism, are predisposed to accept comprehensive dogmas which purport to supply answers to a variety of issues. It is unsurprising, then, that they are more, rather than less likely to succumb to military indoctrination in spite of their almost universal claim to the contrary. Burchard (1954) claims that the chaplain in his "social worker" in preference to his pastoral role, often overidentifies or completely accepts the official military perspective. In other words, as previously stated, individuals adjust their behaviour to suit the demands of their immediate social milieu. The action of the chaplain in reporting the self-confessed homosexual is approved of according to military standards of right behaviour. There is no question of insincerity on the part of those chaplains. Their behaviour is quite correct so long as no outsider alerts them to a discordance between supporting the military in its internal disciplinary role and exercising a caring religious ministry *cura animarum*. The chaplain who finds himself within an organization in which a particular attitude is taken for granted, has been shown to be highly likely to become increasingly more prone to share and uphold its basic assumptions.

The Army is a relatively closed or carceral system. By that is meant that it presents very few options to the individual in terms of roles and behaviour or even the thinking and perceptions a person can recognise and pursue. Shaef and Fassel (1990) have called it an "addictive system". An addictive system, they say, operates from the same characteristics that individual addicts have routinely exhibited. The major defence mechanism of addicts is denial, on the principle that if something does not exist, it simply does not have to be considered. When chaplains will not let themselves see or know that what is happening might be wrong, they pose no threat to the continuation of a potentially dysfunctional system. Without a reminder from the leaders of the Chaplains' Department that chaplains are first and foremost ministers of religion, some chaplains might be in danger of constructing a dishonest system.

Participation in Group Bias

Over the past one hundred and fifty years the growth of a doctrine about society, stemming from a belief in a radical interrelationship between all humans, was derived in part from the Biblical doctrine of the mystical body of Christ and the communion of the saints. Twentieth century wars in particular demonstrated that Christian believers have shown no real reluctance, when called upon by their country, to kill for a cause. That ministers of religion, whose

117

profession it was to preach a gospel of love, could, without censure, advocate the sort of blasphemies which Bishop Winnington Ingram uttered, which were contrary to every precept of Christian teaching and every principle of justice evolved over two thousand years, provides a vivid example of religion as ideology: the deformation of the truth for the sake of a social interest. That army chaplains wittingly or unwittingly engaged to a greater or lesser degree in using their position to promote national wars with the support of religion, cannot be denied.

The aftermath of the two World Wars brought home to many the injustices embodied in societies, spurring an appreciation that Christianity must not concern itself solely with a transcendental reality called salvation, but must necessarily be active in the struggle against social injustices, the evidence of the reality of social sin. The intricacy of social structures and the chaplain's privileged share in an institution whose basic myth must place national loyalty above the claims of the global community, together with the union of Church and State, has not helped many British army chaplains to understand their adopted role in legitimating the status quo, nor to prevent them from using religion as a weapon of social control. O'Keefe (1990:10) exemplifies social sin: "a slaveowner 'of good conscience', who might have acknowledged his or her cruelty to an individual slave, but remain completely inattentive to the evil of the institution of slavery itself." The blurring of the distinction between 'legal' and 'moral' has inclined chaplains, no less than others, to the belief that if they act according to the law they must therefore be acting morally and that an historically legitimate army chaplaincy needs no analysis.

It is not the assertion of this study that army chaplaincy is immoral, but how far short its present manifestation might be from an ideal, could be illustrated by the role of an Eighteenth century clergyman, whose readiness to minister on board a slave ship, with the intention of mitigating the dehumanizing trends built into the legal and highly profitable system, might have won him praise. At that time for a clergyman to have advocated kindness to slaves may have marked him as an enlightened if not Christlike figure, but such an exhortation today would be the expression of a deformed morality, yesterday's charity having rightly become today's justice. This study has illustrated the failure of chaplains to show awareness of the ambivalence of their role, as well as failure to accentuate what is the task of theology, which is to liberate the church's life from various ideologies that distort the Christian message. Army chaplains have exemplified the maxim that if a society maintains that some disvalues are in fact to be valued, the significant members of that society are most likely to accept the disvalues as values. Once more, this perception is made, not to malign chaplains, for I am, and have been a Reserve and Regular Army chaplain for over twenty years, but to show awareness that basic knowledge of good can co-exist with partial blindness to other values, and that the adoption of a particular view of reality takes place through mental processes that remain largely unconscious.

Conclusion

> It cannot be too strongly stated that Christianity and moral theology do not claim to be able to provide easy or straightforward answers to moral problems of great complexity. Moral theology has the much more limited task of trying to teach Christians to think clearly and correctly about moral problems and thus enable them to approach the actual decisions which have to be made with a better hope of being able to find their own right decision and to help other people along the same path. Great harm has been done, and continues to be done by the idea that Christianity can put the world to rights by giving clear and simple answers to complex problems (Waddams, 1960,40)

This study has concentrated upon conflict arising from the exercise of ministry in peace and war by members of the Royal Army Chaplains' Department (RAChD). Simultaneous membership of church or denomination and army has been seen to have posed differing tensions for different churches in a background of taken-for-granted satisfaction by all participating churches in providing chaplains for the organized arm of massive defensive or offensive

119

State violence. Synchronous engagement by two organizations, whose purposes are not immediately reconcilable, have been shown to create tensions from conflicting loyalties. The official goal of the RAChD - to make and sustain Christians - though its manifest function has been seen at the micro level to have been subsumed into a latent function of providing practical support for the specifically military objective of the host organization.

The conflicts besetting army chaplaincy have been shown to have been symptomatic of the imprecision confronting the nature of religious ministry itself . The findings of this study are rooted in the context of the altered status and role of clergymen in British society throughout this century. Reduction in status was mirrored by a proportionate drop in clerical income. Role uncertainty reflected the civilian experience to such a degree that the sociological definition of an occupation, as a definite statement about what its members do in their work, casts serious doubt whether army chaplaincy, especially in wartime, was either a profession or occupation, so varied were the activities of chaplains.

The paradoxically high regard in which chaplains were held by commanders during the period contrasts with the uneasy respect and mild disdain exhibited by soldiers towards them.

> 14th March 1915: Church Parade was in an upper hall of the school at L'Armée. The Padre preached about his 'terrible experience' in having to talk to some men who had been condemned to be shot. Corporal Hughes of C Company, a stout little fellow on patrol, remarked to a friend as he was leaving the hall, "And indeed, it must have been a terrible experience for those poor men to be talked to by a Padre like that." (Dunn, 1994, 124).

Functional analysis of the chaplains' role produced the curious discovery that with the exception of the universally detested Parade Services, little of what many chaplains appear to have done was of a religious nature. The voluntary, amateur, social ministry provided by many Low Church clergymen before World War One, when continued in the trenches, though highly regarded by those who were its beneficiaries, came close to being a substitute rather than an adjunct to specifically spiritual ministry. Engagement in a predominantly spiritual role fell to High Church Anglicans and Roman Catholics, whose theology, combined with a strongly sacramental ministry, contrasted sharply with the well-meaning, generalized beneficence engaged in by other chaplains. Satisfaction with a spiritual ministry, unless allied to the organization of enthusiasm, did not meet the army's ideal of a good chaplain, though at the micro level, such chaplaincy appeared to its observers as a more professional ministry.

At the institutional level has been seen the existence of conflict engendered by rival claims made upon chaplains engaged simultaneously by the chaplain's own church and the army. The unreflective, commonly accepted view of chaplains as clergymen in army uniform, providing simply and solely the same religious ministry as they would in a civilian setting, is rejected as inadequate and uni-dimensional, at variance with the findings of behavioural, psychological and sociological research. Membership of and incorporation into a closed institution, in which a hierarchical order is embodied, is revealed to be a sufficient cause of resocialization, whereby the behaviour of an individual is adjusted to suit the demands of the immediate social milieu. First World War chaplains were socially conditioned unquestioningly to accept as advantageous their membership of the officer class, yet some were conscious that it distanced them from soldiers. The more recent egalitarian climate is not reflected by any altered chaplaincy attitude towards the presumed advantage to ministry accruing from such military status. Socialization and group interest would appear to account for the dominant chaplaincy ethos which simultaneously maintains the unimportance of rank to chaplains with a lively preoccupation with the lifestyle, status and career enhancement within the chaplaincy which promotion provides.

The RAChD reproduces in its membership the fragmented nature of religion in British society, preventing any but the most general directives from chaplaincy leadership on the attainment of its declared objective of making and sustaining Christians. Keen to fulfil that primary role in war and peace, chaplains are influenced by a view of reality which is a function of their social and military conditioning whose influence often increases in proportion to length of service, and has been shown to have determined what in fact they did.

To have singled out notable chaplains who were not in advance of their generation might appear less than scholarly, but was done deliberately and it is believed justifiably, to redress a balance which has presented such chaplains as exemplars of chaplaincy at its best. Illustrations of the adopted role of chaplains as social lubricators, caterers or general social workers and their total failure to exercise a much vaunted role of prophetic ministry, or their presentation of national conflict in terms of religious crusade or Jehad, are made out of an understanding of the powerful but subtle social conditioning at work forming in them the perspective and aims of the dominant organization.

Through a critical organizational perspective has been seen the framework in which army chaplaincy operates. Contentment with what they are permitted to do, in providing ministry from a position of significance from within the military, leads to a suppression of responsibility to contest with the military. The notable discovery that Ackerman, in writing an official history of chaplaincy while still a serving chaplain, excluded available research evidence which would have reflected unfavourably upon US army chaplaincy in Vietnam, supports the findings of this study and those of Burchard (1953) and Zahn (1969) that the exercise of idealistic disloyalty will be subverted by the psychological need of acceptance by the host organization, to which loyalty is owed in return for membership, significance and status. Similar reciprocal exchange for acceptance inhibits vigorous presentation of religion, to all but the few who attend liturgical worship, and has promoted a chaplaincy ethos, unburdened by evidence, which embodies the axiom that the presence of the chaplain alongside soldiers is sufficient to produce an osmotic religious effect upon them.

British army chaplaincy depends for its freedom of operation upon the power structure of the army itself. Though as an institution the Chaplains' Department can easily and briefly state its role to make and sustain Christians, it has engaged in such a plethora of activities under the auspices of chaplaincy, that it is unsurprising that the army itself has continually and incidentally attempted to redefine its purpose for its own, rather than declared chaplaincy ends. The extent to which the chaplaincy in the army has been peripheralized can be drawn from the following Area Objective of the Health and Welfare Department of the Army which declares its aim as follows

> To promote the health and welfare of all military, civilian and dependent members of the Command through the functional responsibility of primary health, and provision and maintenance of secondary health, dental care and spiritual and welfare services.

The dynamic of a favoured relationship between army and chaplaincy persists, but its weakness is as much a function of the disorientation exhibited by chaplains themselves, as the reduction in importance given by society to religion.

> Army combat commanders in the field have fire support coordinators attached to advise them on the best use of artillery fire to support their mission. They have forward air controllers to coordinate the best use of air power. They have an S1 to appraise them of their personnel matters, an S2 to keep them up to speed on enemy intelligence, an S3 to plan and oversee operations, an S4 to ensure the flow of arms, ammunition, POL, food, water, and other essentials and perhaps even an S5 to help with civilian control. And they have, but all too seldom use, what may be their most important advisor of all - their chaplains. (Summers, 1990,7).

Successfully to communicate the message of Christ in a military context will demand a greater awareness than hitherto of the institutional pressures which too readily divert chaplains from their primary religious ministry of preaching the gospel - *cura animarum* - into secondary, secular, albeit laudable, activities.

Chaplains, it would seem, must confront the qualities of ambivalence and paradox in their role, doing justice to the complexity of a ministry that has been shown to be both engaging as well as potentially corrupting. Analysis might oblige the participants to review neat simplisitic categories of good or evil:

> There is some soul of goodness in things evil,
> Would men observingly distil it out.
>
> (Henry V, iv:1)

We merely pose the question: might there be some taint of evil in things good?

APPENDIX

Gulf War Chaplains' Questionnaire

TRAINING/EDUCATION

Using a scale of A to I, indicate your evaluation of the following training and education as it prepared you for service in the Gulf.

A rating of '**A**' means **Very good**
A rating of '**I**' means **Very poor**
A rating of '**E**' means **Fair**

1. Chaplain training (Sandhurst courses, other formal instruction, chaplains' Exercises, etc.):

    Very good   Fair   Very Poor
    A   B   C   D   E   F   G   H   I

2. Military training (other than specifically chaplain training):

    Very good   Fair   Very Poor
    A   B   C   D   E   F   G   H   I

3. Civilian education and training (University, seminary, practical experience as minister, priest):

    Very good   Fair   Very Poor
    A   B   C   D   E   F   G   H   I

4. Which of the following did the most to prepare you for service as a chaplain in the Gulf? Rank order (1 - least important; 5 - most important)

    .... Chaplain training
    .... Military training (other than chaplain)
    .... Seminary
    .... Prior experience as a clergyman
    .... Common sense

5. Should training a chaplain for possible combat situations be changed? How?

RELATIONSHIPS

6. Overall, my commander's (s') relationship with me was: (Tick as many as apply)

a. Friendly   e. Neutral
b. Supportive   f. Hostile
c. Helpful   g. Other (please explain)
d. Business-like

7. Overall, my relationship with my commander (s) was: (Tick as many as apply)

a. Friendly   e. Neutral
b. Supportive   f. Hostile
c. Helpful   g. Other (please explain)
d. Business-like

8. Overall my chaplain assistant's (s') relationship with me was: (Tick as many as apply)

a. Friendly   e. Neutral
b. Supportive   f. Hostile
c. Helpful   g. Other (please explain)
d. Business-like

9. Overall, my relationship with my chaplain assistant (s) was: (Tick as many as apply)

a. Friendly   e. Neutral
b. Supportive   f. Hostile
c. Helpful   g. Other (please explain)
d. Business-like

10. Overall in my unit(s), other commissioned officers' relationships with me were: (Tick as many as apply)

a. Friendly   e. Neutral
b. Supportive   f. Hostile
c. Helpful   g. Other (please explain)
d. Business-like

11. Overall, in my unit(s), my relationships with other commissioned officers were: (Tick as many as apply)

a. Friendly
b. Supportive
c. Helpful
d. Business-like

e. Neutral
f. Hostile
g. Other (please explain)

12. Overall, in my unit(s), non-commissioned officers' relationships with me were: (Tick as many as apply)

a. Friendly
b. Supportive
c. Helpful
d. Business-like

e. Neutral
f. Hostile
g. Other (please explain)

13. Overall, in my unit(s), my relationship with non-commissioned officers was: (Tick as many as apply)

a. Friendly
b. Supportive
c. Helpful
d. Business-like

e. Neutral
f. Hostile
g. Other (please explain)

14. Overall, in my unit, soldiers' relationships with me were: (Tick as many as apply)

a. Friendly
b. Supportive
c. Helpful
d. Business-like

e. Neutral
f. Hostile
g. Other (please explain)

15. Overall, in my unit, my relationships with soldiers were: (Tick as many as apply)

a. Friendly
b. Supportive
c. Helpful
d. Business-like

e. Neutral
f. Hostile
g. Other (please explain)

16. Overall, my senior chaplain's (s') relationship with me was: (Tick as many as apply)
a. Friendly
b. Supportive
c. Helpful
d. Business-like
e. Neutral
f. Hostile
g. Other (please explain)

17. Overall, my relationship with my senior chaplain(s) was: (Tick as many as apply)
a. Friendly
b. Supportive
c. Helpful
d. Business-like
e. Neutral
f. Hostile
g. Other (please explain)

18. Overall, other chaplains (other than senior) relationships with me were: (Tick as many as apply)
a. Friendly
b. Supportive
c. Helpful
d. Business-like
e. Neutral
f. Hostile
g. Other (please explain)

19. Overall, my relationship with other chaplains (other than supervisory) was: (Tick as many as apply)
a. Friendly
b. Supportive
c. Helpful
d. Business-like
e. Neutral
f. Hostile
g. Other (please explain)

20. If you have anything more to say about relationships with any of the people mentioned above or with anyone else, please use the following space to do so.

MINISTRY

21. Rank the following aspects of ministry in order of time spent. (1 - Least Time Spent; 10 - Most Time Spent)
Remember this is about the time you served in the Gulf.
.... a. Sacramental
.... b. Counselling
.... c. "Presence" (visiting troops, going on operations)
.... d. Visitation of sick and wounded
.... e. Worship services
.... f. Memorial services
.... g. Civic action
.... h. Evangelism
.... i. Corresponding with families of service members
.... j. Other (please explain)..

22. Rank the following aspects of ministry in order of importance you placed on them in the **Gulf.** (1 - Least important; 10 - Most important)
.... a. Sacramental
.... b. Counselling
.... c. "Presence" (visiting troops, going on operations)
.... d. Visitation of sick and wounded
.... e. Worship services
.... f. Memorial services
.... g. Civic action
.... h. Evangelism
.... i. Corresponding with families of service members
.... j. Other (please explain)..

23. On the whole, my ministry in the Gulf made me feel: (Tick as many as apply)
.... a. Satisfied
.... b. Overwhelmed
.... c. Able to cope with whatever came up
.... d. Adequate
.... e. Properly utilized
.... f. Underutilized
.... g. Unsure
.... h. Other feelings. Describe..............................

24. Has the Gulf experience changed your ministry?

    …............   a. Yes
    …............   b. No
    …............   c. Unsure
Please explain

25. Did the Gulf experience change your life in other ways? If so, how?

26. Were there any hindrances to your ministry while a chaplain in the Gulf? Please elaborate.

27. Was your faith?   …............ Strengthened
                               …............ Weakened
                               …............ Unchanged
                               …............ Other
Please explain:

28. What were your personal feelings about service in the Gulf?

29. Did your attitude toward the military change as a result of the Gulf experience?   How?

30. Has your attitude toward the chaplaincy changed as a result of the Gulf experience?   How?

31. Has your attitude toward the civilian community changed as a result of the Gulf experience?   How?

32. Overall, what problems were most often brought to you by soldiers in the Gulf?

33. Overall, what problems were most often brought to you by officers in the Gulf?

130

34. Please give two brief narratives of what you consider the most significant events of your Gulf ministry. (These events may or may not be well known. We are concerned primarily with the incidents which, in your memory, were particularly significant during the course of your ministry in the Gulf).

35. If there is anything else you wish to comment on regarding your experiences in the Gulf or your ministry at other military installations during that time period, please feel free to do so. All information is greatly appreciated.

I hereby authorise the Rev S H Louden to publish any of the above material excluding the exceptions stated below:

....
....

Signature ....

Your Help is Needed

If you know of anyone, other than chaplains, who served in the Gulf (commissioned officer, non-commissioned officer, soldier or civilian) or family of servicemen who served in the Gulf who might be willing to comment on chaplain ministry in the Gulf, please list their names and present addresses:

....
....
....
....

If you have any questions or suggestions regarding this study, comment here.

BIBLIOGRAPHY

Ackermann, Henry F, 1989, *He Was Always There: The US Army Chaplain Ministry in the Vietnam Conflict.* Washington: US Gov Printing Office

Baum, Gregory, 1975, *Religion and Alienation: A Theological Reading of Sociology.* New York. Paulist Press

Bennett, Alan, 1991, *Talking Heads.* London, BBC Books

Berger, Peter L, 1963, *Invitation to Sociology: A Humanistic Perspective.* London: Pelican

Berger, Peter and Pinnard, Daniel, 1971, "Military Religion: An Analysis of Educational Material Disseminated by Chaplains." In *Military Chaplains: From a Religious Military to a Military Religion* Ed. Harvey J Cox Jnr. New York. American Report Press

Berger, Peter L & Berger, Brigitte, 1978, *Sociology: A Biographical Approach* Rev. edn Harmondsworth: Penguin

Blackburne, Harry, 1932, *This Also Happened on the Western Front,* London. Hodder & Stoughton

Blair, Duncan, 1954, Leaves from the Journal of a Scottish Padre in the First World War *Chaplains' Department Journal* 8 (1954) 57

Brown, Hedy, 1985, *People, Groups and Society.* Milton Keynes: Open University Press

Bull, Paul B, 1926, A Memorandum on Compulsory Parade Service in Army and Navy, *Chaplains' Department Journal* 2 (1926) 17

Burchard, W Waldo, 1953, *The Role of the Military Chaplain,* Unpublished PhD Dissertation: University of California at Berkley

Chapman, Guy, 1933, *A Passionate Prodigality* 1965 edn

CHB,1989, *Chaplains' Handbook*

Cleroux, Richard, 1996, *The Times* 6th July 1996 p16

Clifford, Joan (Ed.), 1989, *Thank you Padre: Memories of World War 2* London: Fount Paperback

Cox, G Harvey (Ed.), 1971, *Military Chaplains: From a Religious Military to a Military Religion.* New York. America Report Press

Dunn, J.C. (Ed.), 1938, *The War The Infantry Knew 1914-1919,* 1994 edn. London, Abacus

Essame, H, 1952, *The 43 Wessex Division at War 1944-45.* London

Freedman, J L, Sears, D, D, Carlsmith, J M 1981*Social Psychology.* Fourth Edition, New Jersey. Prentice Hall

Gethyn-Jones, Eric, 1988, *A Territorial Army Chaplain in Peace and War: A country cleric in khaki 1938-61.* East Wittering: Gooday Publishers

Graves, Robert, 1929, *Goodbye To All That.*

Gushwa, Robert L, 1977, *The Best and Worst of Times: The United States Army Chaplaincy 1920-1945.* Vol 4 US Government Printing Office

Gwynne, Ll H, 1923, Church of England Organization and Work in the British Expeditionary Force. *Chaplains' Department Journal* 2 (1923) 5

Haigh, H Bryant, 1983, *Men of Faith and Courage: The Official History of New Zealand Army Chaplains.* Auckland: The World Publishers

Hall, R H, 1980, 'Organizational Goals'. In *Organizations as Systems.* Eds Lockett, Martin, Spear Roger. OUP.

Hodge B J and Anthony, W P, 1988, *Organization Theory: An Environmental Approach.* 2 Edn. Allyn and Bacon.

Horne, Jonathan, 1995, *The Best of Good Fellows.* The diaries and memoirs of the Rev C E Doudney. Jonathan Horne Publications.

Horsley Smith, C J, 1978, A Chaplain's Recollections of 1917-1918 *Chaplains' Department Journal 24 (1978) 130*

Hughes, F Ll, 1943, Unpublished letter to DCG, 5 August

1944 a *The Chaplain in Invasion.* Cairo NMP

1944 b, *The Chaplains of the Grand Assault.* A Summary of the Experience in the Field of the Eighth Army Brotherhood of Chaplains. MEF Printing Service

1947, *Notes on Religious Instructions in the British Army.* Bagshot Park

Janowitz, Morris, 1971, *The Professional Soldier: A Social and Political Portrait.* Rev Edn. New York: Free Press Paperback

Janowitz, Morris and Little R.W. 1974, *Sociology and the Military Establishment.* 3 Edn. London, Sage.

Jarvis, A C, 1929, The Place of the Church in the Life of the Army. *Chaplains' Department Journal* 13 (1929) 27

Kerans, Patrick, 1974, *Sinful Social Structures.* New York: Paulist Press

Kung, Hans, 1972, *Why Priests? A Proposal for a New Church Ministry.* New York: Doubleday

Lewis, C S, 1959, *Surprised by Joy.* Fontana Books

Lloyd, G A Lewis, 1950, *The Padre is your Friend.* London: A R Mowbray & Co

Marrin, Albert, 1974, *The Last Crusade: The Church of England and the First World War.* Duke University Press

McGuire, Meredeth B, 1987, *Religion: The Social Context.* 2nd Edn. Wadsworth Inc

McLeish, Robert (ed), 1990, *The Work of Methodist Chaplains in the Armed Forces.* (Unpublished)

McLusky, J Fraser, 1951, *Parachute Padre:* London: SCM Press

Middleton Brumwell, The Rev P, 1943, *The Army Chaplain.* London: Adam and Charles Black

Monyhan, Michael, 1983, *God On Our Side. The British Padre in World War One.* Secker and Warburg

Medhurst, K, and Moyser, G, 1988, *Church and Politics in a Secular Age.* Oxford University Press

Muttram, G R, 1991, *Churches, Chaplains and Chaplaincies* Unpublished MTh Dissertation, Westminster College Oxford

Norton, Herman A, 1977, *Struggling for Recognition: The United States Army Chaplaincy 1791-1865.* Vol 2 US Government Printing Office.

O'Connor, J. John, 1988, A Chaplain Responds. *America* Aug 7/14

O'Keefe, Mark, 1990, *What Are They Saying About Social Sin.* Mahwah NJ: Paulist Press

Oliver, Kenneth, 1986, *Chaplain at War.* Chichester: Angel Press

Palgrave, F T, 1906, *The Golden Treasury of English Songs and Lyrics.* London: Dent

Purcell, William, 1962, *Woodbine Willie.* A Biography. London Hodder & Stoughton

Purves, Libby, 1992, 'Blind eyes and office dogs who never bark' *The Times* 22 June 1992 p16

Report, 1919, *The Army and Religion: An Enquiry and its Bearing upon the Religious Life of the Nation*

Robertson Roland, 1970, *The Sociological Interpretation of Religion.* Oxford: Basil Blackwell

Royal Warrant, 1796, *The Royal Army Chaplains' Department Journal.* 3 (1930), 292

Russell, Anthony, 1984, *The Clerical Profession.* London: SPCK

Schaef, A.W. and Fassel, D.,1990, *The Addictive Organization.* San Francisco, Harper

Schillebeeks, Edward, 1981, *Ministry: Leadership in the Community of Jesus Christ.* New York: Crossroad

Schneider, Stanley, 1989, The Chaplain/Rabbi as a Reducer of Stress. *Journal of Psychology and Judaism* 13(1) Spring 1989

Semphill, G D, 1926, 'Recruiting'. *Chaplains' Department Journal* 2 (1926) 17

Shils, Edward, 1975, 'Centre and Periphery'. In *Society and the Social Sciences.* Ed. David Potter Open University Press

Sinclair, Ronald, 1941, *A Religion for Battledress.* London: A Mowbray & Co.

Smyth VC, Sir John, 1968, *In This Sign Conquer. The story of the Army Chaplains* A R Mowbray & Co Ltd

Steven, Walter T, 1948, *In This Sign.* Canadian Chaplaincy Service Toronto: The Ryerson Press

Stover, Earl F, 1977, *Up From Handymen: The United States Army Chaplaincy 1865-1920*. Vol 3 US Government Printing Office

Stubblefield, Jerry M, 1987, *A Church Ministering to Adults*. Nashville. Broadman Press

Studdert Kennedy, G A, 1919, *Rough Talks by a Padre*. Hodder & Stoughton

Summers, Harry G. Jr., 1990, The Chaplain as Moral Touchstone, *Military Chaplains Review*, Spring, 7.

Tavard, George H, 1983, *A Theology for Ministry*. Dublin: Dominican Publications

Thompson, Parker C, 1978, *From its European Antecedents To 1791. The United States Army Chaplaincy* Vol 1 US Government Printing Office

Towler, Robert, 1985, *The Need for Certainty*. London: Routledge & Keegan Paul

Tuckey, J G, 1926, Editorial. *Chaplains' Department Journal* 2 (1926) 19

Venzke, Roger R, 1977, *Confidence in Battle. Inspiration in Peace. The United States Army Chaplaincy 1945-1975* Vol 5. US Government Printing Office

Waddams, Herbert, 1960, A New Introduction to Moral Theology

Watkins, Owen Spencer, 1906, *Soldiers and Preachers Too*. London: Charles H Kelly

Whitlow, Maurice, 1938, *J Taylor Smith: Everybody's Bishop* London: The Lutterworth Press

Wilcocks, J Arthur, 1943, Unpublished Letters to Hughes, FL1 Chaplains' Department Records.

Wilkinson, Alan, 1978, *The Church of England and the First World War*. London: SPCK

1986, *Dissent or Conform? War, Peace and the English Churches 1900-1945*. London: SCM Press

William, George H, 1971, The Chaplaincy in the Armed Forces of the United States. In *Military Chaplains: From a Religious Military to Military Religion*. (Ed) Harvey, G Cox. American Report Press

Willis, Leonard, 1986, *None Had Lances. The Story of the 24th Lancers*. Chippenham: Picton Print

Wright, Ronald Selby, 1943, *Let's Ask the Padre: Some Broadcast Talks*. London: Oliver & Boyce

Young, Francis & Wilson, Kenneth, 1986, *Focus on God*. London: Epworth Press

Zahn, Gordon H, 1969, *Chaplains in the RAF: A Study in Role Tension*. Manchester University Press

1971, "Sociological Impressions of the Chaplaincy". In *Military Chaplains: From a Religious Military to a Military Religion*. (Ed.) Harvey G Cox. American Report Press

INDEX